THE PUGINS
AND THE
CATHOLIC MIDLANDS

Dedicated to my father,
Conal McDonagh O'Donnell MBE, TD
(1915–1996)
of Stone, Staffordshire, 1934–1948
RIP

Publication of this book was made possible by a grant from the Scouloudi Foundation in association with the Institute of Historical Research, and by the award of a Stroud Bursary by the Society of Architectural Historians of Great Britain.

THE PUGINS
AND THE
CATHOLIC MIDLANDS

Roderick O'Donnell

GRACEWING

ARCHDIOCESE OF BIRMINGHAM
HISTORICAL COMMISSION

First published in 2002
jointly by

Gracewing
2 Southern Avenue
Leominster
Herefordshire
HR6 0QF

Archdiocese of Birmingham
35 Kenilworth Road
Leamington Spa
Warwickshire
CV32 6JG

GRACEWING ISBN 0 85244 567 9
ARCHDIOCESE OF BIRMINGHAM HISTORICAL COMMISSION
ISBN 1 871269 17 8

Typeset by Action Publishing Technology Ltd,
Gloucester GL1 5SR

Printed by MPG Books Ltd,
Bodmin PL31 1EG

CONTENTS

ABBREVIATIONS

BAA: Birmingham Archdiocesan Archives, Cathedral House, St Chad's Queensway, Birmingham

OJ: *London and Dublin Orthodox Journal*

Wedgwood, *Pugin Family:* Alexandra Wedgwood, *Catalogue of the Architectural Drawings in the Victoria and Albert Museum: A. W. N. Pugin and the Pugin Family* (1985)

ILLUSTRATIONS

BLACK AND WHITE
1. A. W. N. Pugin, 'The Present Revival of Christian Architecture', frontispiece to *The Apology for the Revival of Christian Architecture* (1843).
2. (i) A. W. N. Pugin, *The Glossary of Ecclesiastical Ornament* (1844), frontispiece.
   (ii) Anonymous sketch, St Cuthbert's College, Ushaw.
3. A. W. N. Pugin, 'Contrasted residences for the Poor': *Contrasts* (1841).
4. Alton Towers Chapel: interior reconstruction by Revd M. Fisher, 1998. Photograph – courtesy of M. Fisher.
5. The funeral of the Earl of Shrewsbury, from *The Illustrated London News*, 1852. Photograph – courtesy of Revd M. Fisher.
6. Alton Hospital of St John the Baptist
   (i) The chapel, from *Present State*.
   (ii) A. W. N. Pugin's bird's-eye view from *Present State* (1843).
7. Alton Castle from the south, 1963. Photograph – courtesy of The Royal Commission on the Historical Monuments of England.
8. Banbury, Church of St John the Baptist
   (i) The interior *c.* 1910, showing fittings attributed to Pugin.
   (ii) Church interior.
   Photographs – courtesy of Fr Bede Walsh, PP.

9. Belmont, The Abbey Church of St Michael and All Angels
   (i)   The Abbey Church and monastic buildings.
   (ii) The nave and crossing.
   Photographs – courtesy of the Abbot of Belmont.
10. Belmont, The Abbey Church of St Michael and All Angels
    (i)   Monastic choir and sanctuary.
    (ii) High altar and reredos, carved by R. L. Boulton.
    Photographs – courtesy of the Abbot of Belmont.
11. Birmingham, the Bishop's House (demolished): Pugin's drawing from *Present State*.
12. Birmingham, St Chad's Cathedral: Pugin's rood screen. Photograph – courtesy of English Heritage, National Monuments Record.
13. Birmingham, St Chad's Cathedral
    (i)   The Sanctuary, 1904. Photograph – copy of a print taken from a glass negative – Birmingham Archdiocesan Archives, P1/59.
    (ii) The exterior *c.* 1978. Photograph – courtesy of The Courtauld Institute of Art.
14. St Mary's College, Oscott: Pugin's etching of the interior (1837).
15. (i)   Handsworth, Convent of Mercy: the chapel *c.* 1935.
    (ii) Nechells, St Joseph: the chancel.
    (iii) Brewood, St Mary: the nave arcade and south aisle.
    (iv) Brewood, St Mary: the font. Photograph – Graham Miller.
16. Cheadle, St Giles
    (i)   The east end. Photograph – courtesy of English Heritage, National Monuments Record.
    (ii) Pugin's plan from *Present State*.
17. Derby, St Mary
    (i)   From Bridge Gate.
    (ii) Interior.
    Photographs – courtesy of English Heritage, National Monuments Record.

COLOUR
1. A. W. N. Pugin (1812–1852), painted by J. R. Herbert – oil on canvas – in a frame made by J. G. Crace to Pugin's design (now at the Palace of Westminster). Photograph – Graham Miller.
2. John Talbot, 16th Earl of Shrewsbury and Waterford. Portrait – oil on canvas – painted by Carl Blass *c.* 1851, now at Carlton Towers, Yorkshire. The Earl is holding the text of his letter to Lord John Russell (see pp. 28, 40 n.142). Photograph – Jim Nancarrow, 2002; courtesy of the Beaumont Trustees, and the Duke of Norfolk.
3. (i) The Alton Towers high altar *c.* 1840.
   (ii) Detail showing the 16th Earl of Shrewsbury with his patron, St John the Baptist.
   Photographs – Graham Miller.
4. (i) St Mary's College, Oscott (1834–38) by Messrs Roberts, architects.
   (ii) The chapel as furnished by Pugin.
   Photographs – the author.
5. The Church of St Giles, Cheadle (1840–46): the nave. Photograph – Graham Miller.
6. The Church of St Giles, Cheadle
   (i) The north or Lady aisle: wall painting and window – the Seven Corporal Works of Mercy – by William Wailes.
   (ii) 'Burying the Dead' from the Seven Corporal Works of Mercy.
   Photographs – Graham Miller.
7. St Giles, Cheadle
   (i) The Rood.
   (ii) Reredos detail.
   Photographs – the author.
8. (i) St Giles, Cheadle: the pulpit and Lady altar.
   (ii) The Blessed Sacrament chapel screen.
   Photographs – the author.
9. (i) Chalice (Church of Our Lady, Blackmore Park, Worcestershire) by Hardman & Co. to a Pugin design. This example has not yet been dated or

ACKNOWLEDGEMENTS

I was educated in the Midlands in the 1960s and first knew many of these buildings just before the Second Vatican Council. A certain nostalgia for an under-regarded architectural culture therefore helped to motivate my Cambridge PhD thesis 'Roman Catholic Church Architecture in Great Britain and Ireland 1829–1878' (1983), for which much of the research for this book was undertaken. Some of the churches described I have not seen since that time; I am therefore very grateful to Brian Andrews who, in preparing the exhibition catalogue *Creating a Gothic Paradise, Pugin at the Antipodes* (2002), revisited many with my draft text during the spring of 2000. The Revd Michael Fisher, author of *Pugin-land* (2002), also gave me many prompts, visited Burton Manor, Stafford, for me, and generously provided photographs, as well as the drawing of his reconstruction of the cast end of the chapel of Alton Towers. Because so many churches have been altered almost out of recognition, access to historic photographs has been essential. Paul Atterbury provided generous access to the photographs commissioned for the 1994 exhibition, *Pugin: A Gothic Passion*, many taken by Graham Miller, and others have been garnered from historic collections (St Cuthbert's College, Ushaw, Mercy Convent, Handsworth, Mount St Bernard Abbey, the Myers Family Trust) and the Squire de Lisle (Leicestershire), who are all gratefully acknowledged. The National Monuments Record, Swindon, and its staff have been very generous in extending to me the privileges usually given to those publishing for English Heritage. Other collections which have provided historic photographs are the Archdiocese of Birmingham (The Revd Dr

John Sharp); St John the Baptist, Banbury (Fr Bede Walsh);
Belmont Abbey (Abbot Paul Stonham and Dom Peter Madden,
OSB); KADOC, Catholic University Leuven, Belgium (photo-
graph Luc Vints); Ratcliffe College (Sian Truszkowska and
Bro. Nigel Cave, IC); Stafford Grammar School; Stanbrook
Abbey; St Mary's Abbey, Oulton. Individual photographs have
been supplied by the Revd Brendan Blundell, OFM, Michael
Fisher, and Jim Nancarrow. The Revd B. Doolan, Dean of St
Chad's Cathedral, and Sr Mary Barbara, archivist Handsworth
Mercy Convent, both answered queries or made themselves
available; Dr John Martin Robinson arranged access to Carlton
Towers. Individual comments on the text have been made by Dr
Judith Champ, Dom Michael Evans, OSB and the Revd Anthony
Symondson, SJ. Certain bibliographical references have been
checked by Dom Daniel Rees, OSB, librarian at Downside
Abbey. I am grateful to Professor Jack Scarisbrick, Chairman of
the Archdiocese of Birmingham Historical Commission, at
whose suggestion this volume has been written. For further
work on the text my warm thanks are to my colleagues on the
Archdiocese of Birmingham Historic Churches Committee:
Michael Greenslade, editor of the Archdiocese Historical
Commission series, and the diocesan archivist, the Revd Dr
John Sharp, who have been asked to provide much patient edito-
rial and critical comment; the same thanks are also owed to my
publisher Tom Longford, and the publishing manager at
Gracewing, Jo Ashworth. Professor Andrew Saint and Sandra
Wedgwood (Lady Wedgwood) have over many years given me
support and encouragement, as have fellow members of the
Pugin Society, notably Catriona Blaker, Rosemary Hill and Tim
Brittain-Catlin. Dr Simon Thurley, the Chief Executive of
English Heritage, kindly agreed to write the foreword. My final
and warmest thanks are to those who give me the most support:
Charles Plante and Teddy O'Donnell.

Roderick O'Donnell
Easter 2002.

FOREWORD

The former Catholic chapel at Rotherwas near Hereford is a remarkable and unexpected building to be in the guardianship of English Heritage. This late medieval church with its remarkable roof of 1589 and seventeenth-century tower tells a romantic story of a private chapel kept in Catholic hands over the centuries, a place of Recusancy and survival. Its restoration after 1868 by E. W. Pugin and later by his brother Peter Paul who added the apse, altars, stained glass and statuary, is a fine example of the energies and scholarship of the Gothic Revival and might perhaps have qualified it for inclusion in this book. It is also an example of how the character and use of buildings change, and how as conservationists we value the surviving narrative of such changes.

Rotherwas is unusual in being a Catholic chapel maintained on behalf of the Secretary of State for the Department of Culture, Media and Sport by English Heritage as a monument. Happily most churches are still used for worship and looked after by their congregations. At English Heritage we are only too aware of the great strains this often places on the resources of the communities responsible for their upkeep, and the inadequacy of the financial support we have been able to offer them. English Heritage is even more aware of the threat to this great patrimony posed by the closure of churches and convents, and of the importance of properly informed decision making. What we can offer in abundance is expertise and advice, so that for example Dr O'Donnell, as a member of the Archdiocese of Birmingham Historic Churches Committee, brings his knowledge to bear locally on the many listed and conservation area churches which the diocese and the religious orders maintain. Rory O'Donnell, an Inspector of Historic Buildings at English Heritage, is a noted expert on the architectural setting of Catholic worship of this period in the British Isles, and his expertise is often called upon by our regional offices at Birmingham, Manchester, Newcastle and elsewhere. This book is an important contribution to architectural history, to Catholic and to Victorian studies, and I warmly recommend it.

Simon Thurley
Chief Executive, English Heritage
London
21 August 2002

INTRODUCTION

August Welby Northmore Pugin (1812–1852) was the only
son of the French émigré Charles Pugin and Catherine
Welby.[1] He was educated in his father's drawing office, a
powerhouse of research into the architectural sources of the
Gothic Revival, where his brilliant draughtsmanship developed. He then passed straight into the raffish world of the
theatre, stage design and furniture manufacture. The loss of
his first wife and his father and a bankruptcy sobered him but
not his enthusiasms, and his conversion to Catholicism in 1835
gave him a new raison d'être, which was to be a church architect. He was unimpressed with the buildings and tone of
Regency Catholicism in London. Pugin was an architectural
reformer and propagandist who shook off the habits of the
Regency architectural world to emerge with a greater, more
'Victorian' earnestness of purpose. He almost single-handedly
prevailed upon not only the Catholics but also Anglicans to
build churches only in the Gothic style, and according to rigid
formulae which he laid down.[2] It became almost a heresy to
build in the classical or as he called it the 'Pagan' style; as the
historian David Watkin, reflecting on the impact Pugin's challenge to the classical architectural system in place since the
Renaissance, has observed: 'Pugin claimed ... the same
doctrinal justification for the forms of church architecture as
for the truths of the Church's teachings ... a unique heresy
which the Church might well have condemned had she thought
about it.'[3]

Hardly yet qualified even to call himself an architect in 1837, he quickly assembled a team consisting of the builder George Myers, the potter Herbert Minton, and the Hardmans for metalwork and stained glass, so that he was soon able to claim to estimate for building and furnishing churches (this latter a particular obsession) for sums at least one third less than previously. Pugin was therefore a seminal figure not only in the mid-Victorian applied arts but also in a wider reform movement to be articulated through Gothic Revival principles, that was to incorporate not only architects but also critics such as Ruskin and William Morris, even if they did not acknowledge it. As designer of much of the interior decoration of the rebuilt Houses of Parliament, he is literally part of the national fabric since much of the stained glass, the metalwork and the floor tiles of the new Palace of Westminster (begun 1840) were made to Pugin's design in the Midlands.[4]

From 1838 Pugin became architect by appointment to the Catholic Revival in the large Midland Vicariate presided over by Bishop Walsh, from 1840 divided into two as the Eastern and Central Districts, and the latter from 1850 into the Birmingham and Nottingham dioceses. The Catholicism of the Midlands did not have the large numbers to be found in the North-West or in London, but its foundations were stronger: recusant families had kept the faith alive in Warwickshire and Staffordshire, and by 1688 town congregations were identifiable in Birmingham, Derby and elsewhere. Houses of religious, schools and even a seminary were already well established by 1829; Pugin was usually building for well-established congregations and hardly ever for the newly arriving Irish. By contrast, the overnight growth of the Catholic Revival in Leicestershire was almost single-handedly the work of one man, the convert squire Ambrose Phillipps, who began afresh rather than expanding on the existing historic Dominican missions in Hinckley and Leicester. It was in these Catholic Midlands that some of Pugin's finest buildings and certainly his most fruitful friendships, both lay and clerical, were developed. Beginning with the lay Catholic leader the 16th Earl of Shrewsbury, Pugin quickly added contacts and friendships with the Hardmans, metalwork manufacturers of Birmingham, and Ambrose Phillipps in Leicestershire, all laymen with specific views on the how the Catholic Church in England should be reorganized. The lay aspect is worth remarking on: other publications in the Archdiocese of Birmingham Historical Commission's series have been about the clergy; this is the first to deal with the role and impact of a layman on the Catholic Revival.

Pugin was an inveterate traveller, and as the railways expanded he characterized himself in 1841 as 'a Locomotive being always flyin [*sic*] about'.[5] Although he lived in Ramsgate from 1843, much of his business was in the Midlands, and he practised on a national scale. He came to bury his second wife in St Chad's Cathedral, and after his unexpected death at the age of forty his widow and family moved to 44 Frederick St, Birmingham, at the invitation of John Hardman. His son Edward began to practise as an architect from Birmingham, later re-establishing himself at Ramsgate, London, Liverpool and Dublin. Edward Pugin also died young, aged forty-one, in 1875, but the national scale of the practice was continued by his brother and partner Peter Paul (1851–1904).

The first biography of Pugin was published in 1861, but it was not authorized by his family. The dispersal of his papers has since made the task more difficult and subsequent biographies by Michael Trappes Lomax (1932) and by Phoebe Stanton (1971) have not stood the test; there is still no authoritative monograph on him. However, led by the Metalwork, Furniture and Woodwork Departments at the Victoria and Albert Museum, different specialists have published on many aspects of Pugin, particularly his manuscripts and his work in the applied arts. The *doyenne* of Pugin studies, Alexandra Wedgwood, has edited the catalogues not only of his drawings at the Royal Institute of British Architects and the Victoria and Albert Museum, but also his diary; the late Clive Wainwright masterminded the exhibitions 'Pugin: a Gothic Passion' (1994) at the Victoria and Albert Museum and 'Pugin, Master of the Gothic Revival' (1995) at the Bard Graduate Centre, New York, and edited (with Paul Atterbury) a lavishly illustrated set of essays for the first and further essays and a catalogue for the second. Margaret Belcher has published the first of a multi-volume set of Pugin's *Collected Letters* and Rosemary Hill is writing a 'critical biography' of Pugin. Brian Andrews has mounted the exhibition 'Pugin at the Antipodes' with a catalogue in 2002. Important local studies have been written by the Revd Michael Fisher, including *Pugin-land* (2002). This study has not been able to draw on these last two publications.

Many of Pugin's buildings, and some by his sons, are now listed 'as of special architectural or historic interest'; they are therefore protected in planning law from unauthorized alteration or demolition. For churches in use, each diocese has set up an Historic Churches Committee to cover listed or conservation area buildings, and they must balance 'pastoral' with 'conservation' issues before them, so that the iconoclasm at the chapel of Grace Dieu Manor in 1965 or the radical stripping out at St Chad's Cathedral, Birmingham, in 1967, would now be unthinkable. However, there is no such regime to consider options where original uses cease, such as at Cotton Hall in Staffordshire when Cotton College closed; uncertainty now hangs over Stanbrook Abbey in Worcestershire, since the nuns have announced their intention to move. Many parishes struggle heroically to keep their buildings in repair and only few, such as St Giles at Cheadle, have qualified for grant-aid support. A thriving Pugin Society is based at Ramsgate in Kent, where the Landmark Trust, supported by the Heritage Lottery Fund and English Heritage, has bought Pugin's own house and is appealing for funds to restore it.

This book is a contribution towards the understanding of the Pugins as Catholics, an aspect largely omitted from what one might call the 'V & A school' of Pugin studies, as Fr Anthony Symondson, SJ has noted.[6] As well as a discussion of the architectural evidence of the Catholic Revival, a gazetteer of buildings from Alton Towers in Staffordshire to Wymeswold in Leicestershire shows the breadth of A. W. Pugin's reach. The story is continued to cover the work of his sons Edward and Peter Paul. This book also commemorates the one hundred and fiftieth anniversary of the death of Pugin's patron, the Earl of Shrewsbury, as well as that of A. W. Pugin himself.

Notes

1. B. Ferrey, *Recollections of A. N. Welby [sic] Pugin, and his Father, Augustus Pugin* (1861); R. Hill, 'A. C. Pugin', *Burlington Magazine* 1114, vol. CXXXVIII (January 1996), pp. 11–19.
2. R. O'Donnell, '"Blink [him] by silence"?: the Cambridge Camden Society and A. W. N. Pugin', in C. Webster and J. Elliot (eds), *'A Church as it should be': The Cambridge Camden Society and its Influence* (Stamford, 2001), pp. 98–120.
3. D. J. Watkin, *Morality and Architecture* (Oxford, 1977), p. 3.
4. C. and J. Riding, *The Houses of Parliament: History, Art, Architecture* (2000), especially A. Wedgwood, 'The New Palace of Westminster', pp. 113–35.
5. Pugin to David Charles Read, 14 January 1841, in M. Belcher (ed.), *The Collected Letters of A. W. N. Pugin*, I (Oxford, 2001), p. 193.
6. A. Symondson, SJ, 'Pugin at the V & A Museum: a missed opportunity', in *Apollo*, 140 (January 1995), 54–5.

THE PUGINS AND THE CATHOLIC MIDLANDS

Before he became a Catholic, A. W. N. Pugin's reaction to Birmingham was damning: 'that most detestable of all detestable places – Birmingham, where Greek buildings and smoking chimneys, Radicals and Dissenters are blended together'.[1] But Pugin the Catholic convert architect was to find in the Catholic Midlands his best friends, patrons and supporters, an association perhaps as unexpected as was to be that of Newman himself. At critical times he and his family turned to the Midlands. In the Earl of Shrewsbury's private chapel at Alton Towers Pugin organized the elaborate liturgical reception into the Church of his second wife in 1839.[2] Five years later the Earl attended the same Louisa Pugin's equally elaborate funeral at Birmingham, at which no fewer than seven Catholic bishops were present.[3] It was to Birmingham on Pugin's tragic death in 1852 that his widow and five children came, under the protection of the Hardman family. Although his eldest son, Edward, left Birmingham for London in 1856, the Catholic Midlands continued to provide the practice with some important commissions, particularly from the Benedictine Order, for whom another son, Peter Paul, worked into the twentieth century.

THE ROLE AND STATUS OF THE ARCHITECT

Pugin was both a convert and an architect, and emphatically in that order. His announcement to the Salisbury antiquary

William Osmond in 1834 of his decision to become a Catholic was made in the expectation that Catholic church-building was on the increase: 'I feel perfectly convinced that the Roman Catholic Church is the only true one in which the grand and sublime style of church architecture can ever be restored. A very good chapel is now building in the North, and when it is complete, I certainly think I shall recant.'[4] Pugin's study of new Catholic church-building was indicative of his intention to dominate it by establishing a national reputation and by excluding non-Catholics. Until this date commissions for Catholic churches, if ambitious enough to involve an architect, were as likely to go to local non-Catholics such as Thomas Rickman, the architect of St Mary's, Redditch (1833–4).[5] Even a Catholic already prominent as a local architect, such as Joseph Aloysius Hansom (1803–1882), the designer of Birmingham Town Hall (1832–4), did not become involved in Catholic churchwork until later in the 1830s.[6] The convert the Hon. and Revd George Spencer, a priest since 1832 and to become better known as the Venerable Ignatius Spencer, CP, offered a commission to the Protestant Edward Blore, whom his brother, Earl Spencer, had recently employed.[7]

Pugin was now to introduce a confessional qualification and claim a new significance for the architect, who was no longer to be a mere agent of the patrons or clergy, but the arbiter of cost, scale, style, furnishing and liturgy. He brought into the debate on the Catholic Revival in England strictly technical questions of church design, decoration and function. Although Pugin's meticulous antiquarian standards were far removed from the realities of most Catholic missions, his arguments were immediately endorsed by the leading bishop, Thomas Walsh of the Midland District, and the leading Catholic layman, the Earl of Shrewsbury, both of whom Pugin met in 1837. Allied to these men, he made himself architect almost by appointment to the Catholic Church in England, and his name was associated with almost all new architectural projects, to the exclusion of those architects who had been in Catholic practice before him. Pugin's stylistic revolution dramatically distinguished Catholic church architecture from that of the Anglican Church, of Nonconformity and of the Catholic architecture of his predecessors. It demonstrated it to be that of a Church rather than a sect. His influence went further and banished overnight the classical style from Catholic church architecture. Combined with the support of key patrons, architectural publication and journalism gave Pugin the means to dominate Catholic architectural practice from 1837.[8]

PUGIN'S EARLY JOURNALISM AND EARLY PATRONS

Pugin's journalism seems to have initiated the custom whereby architects published descriptions of their own work in the Catholic press. The earliest was Pugin's own apologia for his churches at Uttoxeter, the first to be begun,[9] and at Solihull, the first to be opened.[10] His *Contrasts or a parallel between the noble edifices of the fourteenth and fifteenth centuries and similar buildings of the present day* ... (1836), a great anti-Reformation broadside, was published privately and did not begin to attract the notice of the Catholic press until 1837.[11]

As well as his own new churches, Pugin was involved with the refurbishing of existing Catholic churches which his publications now showed to be ritually and stylistically inadequate. One of the most influential of these churches was the chapel of Grace Dieu Manor, Leicestershire, opened in 1834 and extended in 1837 by the convert Ambrose Phillipps. Neither the 1834 nor the 1837 press reports named the architect, William Railton, who was to be replaced by Pugin for the alterations of 1839 and an almost complete rebuilding in 1848.[12] Pugin's most dramatic journalism concerned the foundation and consecration of churches. During the first two years of his Catholic church practice he made a series of liturgical and architectural *coups-de-théâtre* which were quite unknown to English Catholics beforehand and which explain much of his early impact on patrons and clergy. He insisted on 'correct' vestments, music and liturgy at the opening ceremonies of his churches, as at St

Mary's, Derby, in 1839, when there was a dramatic confrontation over the substitution of a mixed choir of professional singers, Beethoven and a 'band', for choir and plain chant. This was not simply an intemperate outburst but a necessary tactical gesture. Pugin would not countenance the use of the Gothic vestments which Lord Shrewsbury had intended to give in such a liturgical setting, so Bishop Walsh had to doff the Gothic cloth of gold vestments and with these in their possession Lord Shrewsbury and Pugin left before the ceremony started.[13] Like so much of his style, the Gothic chasuble and the full medieval surplice quickly became an issue between Pugin and his opponents. Unsuccessful attempts were made to ban both, by Bishop Baines in 1839[14] and by Wiseman just before Pugin's death in 1852.[15]

Before Pugin, the ceremonies for the foundation and opening of new churches were primarily occasions not for liturgical display but to pay tribute to local patrons or local liberal Protestants. Pugin's description of the Jesuit church at Hereford, St Francis Xavier (1837–9), attacked this practice as well as the church's neo-classical style and provided the occasion for a comparison with the church which he himself designed at Uttoxeter.[16] In November 1839 the church at Halifax was opened, with furnishings and decorations given gratis by Pugin, and advertised as such.[17] Pugin's derogatory comments on the work of contemporary Catholic architects were equally outspoken even before he began to practise on his own. He heaped ridicule on London's Catholic chapels: 'Warwick Street a Concert Room, Lincoln's Inn Fields dark and grated like a chapel for convicts. Moorfields like a theatre ... the production of a Protestant architect.'[18]

AN 'ENGLISH' CATHOLIC CHURCH?

The Catholic Church which Pugin had joined in 1835 was to be described by later commentators as 'old Catholic', and it was ripe for revivification. Pugin conceived of an 'English' Catholic Church and spoke of 'our ancestors ... not Roman

Catholics [but] English Catholics'.[19] This was quite distinct from the conservatism of the 'old Catholics' and the later Roman enthusiasts. Pugin's authority as architectural and indeed liturgical impresario to the Catholic Church from the time of the consecration of the chapel at Oscott in 1838 to the opening of St George's Cathedral, Southwark, in 1848 was to be largely unchallenged by either the clergy or other Catholic architects. He published sixty-three of his own buildings in two articles (1841–2) to be republished in 1843 as *The Present State of Ecclesiastical Architecture in England*, and in his *An Apology for the Revival of Christian Architecture* (1843) the frontispiece, 'The present revival of Christian architecture', showed twenty-four of thirty church commissions since 1835. The book was dedicated to the Earl of Shrewsbury, whose gift of the new church of St Giles at Cheadle (1840–6) was to be the quintessential expression of this 'English Catholicism', a development which had links with the Anglican Oxford Movement.

That Pugin was achieving something quite new was immediately recognized by an influential visitor from Rome, Dr Nicholas Wiseman, Rector of the English College. Preaching at the opening of Pugin's St Mary's, Derby, in 1839, he stated that it 'will fix the decided transition from chapel to church architecture amongst us'.[20] For Wiseman, the Catholics had left the gloomy catacombs of their 'chapels' for the daylight of churches. If Pugin's impression on a Roman visitor was dramatic, for English Catholics and for those outside the Church it was even stronger. His success was astonishing: from 1838 only in very exceptional circumstances were churches to be in any other style than the Puginesque Gothic. He 'established a new model, almost a new building type, quite discontinuous with Georgian church architecture'.[21] And it was in the Midlands that, in Wiseman's opinion, the 'decisive transition from chapel to church architecture' was to be made, not in the numerically more important Catholic areas such as Lancashire and London. Pugin now sought out Catholic circles in 'Birmingham and other Midland Cyclopean towns', the importance of which Wiseman realized on this visit.[22] Pugin reached a still wider audience than the Catholic Midlands through meeting the Earl of Shrewsbury.

JOHN TALBOT, EARL OF SHREWSBURY AND WATERFORD

John Talbot, 16th Earl of Shrewsbury and Waterford (1791–1852), was the acknowledged lay leader of English Catholicism, in default of his less zealous contemporaries the 12th and 13th Dukes of Norfolk.[23] Pugin first travelled to Shrewsbury's seat, Alton Towers in Staffordshire, in June 1837, returning there in August; on 31 October he noted in his diary 'began Alton Towers'.[24] Pugin was probably introduced to the Earl through his chaplain, the antiquarian Dr Daniel Rock,[25] to whom he had sent a copy of *Contrasts* in 1836.[26] Shrewsbury had not encountered the enthusiasm and conviction displayed by the convert Pugin among the architects brought up as Catholics whom he had previously employed. Pugin had a profound influence on the Earl, through his antiquarian scholarship, his liturgical convictions and his deep sense of the emotional power of architecture. Shrewsbury proved to be Pugin's greatest patron, not only at Alton Towers but for church commissions throughout the Midlands.

The importance of Alton Towers in Catholic affairs was acknowledged: Wiseman made his way in 1835 to 'the princely towers and enchanted gardens of Alton ... I intend to quarter myself on such of the nobility and gentry of these realms as can sufficiently appreciate the honour.'[27] The Earl's house parties at Alton Towers were like a Catholic summer school. Pugin's first visit was undertaken perhaps with more humility than that of Wiseman but with equal guile: here Pugin hoped to further his career by meeting Catholic patrons and clergy. Pugin's lengthy visits, prompted by his professional involvement with the Earl, ensured his inclusion in the most exalted house parties, with guests such as Queen Adelaide, widow of William IV, and the French Legitimist Pretender, Henri de France, Comte de Chambord.[28] A

sequence of Alton meetings and friendships laid the foundation of Pugin's considerable Irish practice through John
Hyacinth Talbot, Member of Parliament for Waterford.[29]
Shrewsbury later chose to summer abroad, claiming to save
£2,000 which could be devoted to church-building.[30]

THE CHURCH PATRONAGE OF THE EARL OF SHREWSBURY

With the succession of John Talbot to his uncle's titles and property in 1827 came immediate responsibilities to Catholic
missions historically supported by the Talbot family. Not only
was a chapel maintained at Alton Towers, but there were also
missions at Cheadle, Uttoxeter and elsewhere in Staffordshire,
and more distantly in Cheshire, Oxfordshire, Shropshire and
Warwickshire. In 1827 Shrewsbury rescued St Peter's, Birmingham, from debts incurred through the ill-advised building
improvements of the priest Thomas McDonnell.[31] Shrewsbury
provided cash for the church at Leek (1828-9)[32] and built the
substantial church of SS Peter and Paul and presbytery at
Newport, Shropshire (1832-3),[33] a Talbot mission since the
seventeeth century; the architect was Joseph Potter. In 1833 the
large, free-standing private chapel at Alton Towers was opened,
replacing a smaller chapel in the house.[34] With the advent of
Pugin in 1837 Shrewsbury's gifts became more generous,
financing complete new churches at Uttoxeter (1838-9), Alton
village and Cheadle, both begun in 1840, and elsewhere in the
Midlands, London and Ireland. It is clear from their correspondence that Shrewsbury took an active part in his churches,
suggesting a separate Blessed Sacrament chapel at Cheadle
(which Pugin called 'an admirable idea of your Lordship. When
I see a good thing stated I am the first to adopt it.')[35] and the use
of alabaster at St John's Hospital in Alton and elsewhere ('the
alabaster answers admirably for the altar . . . I am so glad your
Lordship thought of using it.').[36]

Previous architects such as Potter were dismissed, and from
1837 no church project with which Shrewsbury was involved

went forward without Pugin's appointment as architect as almost his proprietary right. Shrewsbury's practice was to offer sums of money to churches initiated by others, but conditional on Pugin's appointment; Pugin thus secured many more commissions than those in Shrewsbury's direct gift. John Hall, the missioner at Macclesfield, Cheshire, from 1821 until 1857, was a priest of more than usual energy. By the late 1830s he had built two new chapels for his mission; typically, one was a simple classical building incorporating a school, the work of a Liverpool architect. But Hall's next church, St Alban's, Macclesfield (1839–41), was by contrast Gothic, neo-medieval in plan and highly ambitious: it was 128 feet long and housed 800 worshippers.[37]

The explanation, of course, was the intervention of Shrewsbury and Pugin. Although the Earl gave only £1,000 and some furnishings to the church, which cost £8,000 overall, he nevertheless wrote to the Vicar Apostolic of the Northern District, John Briggs, on 18 September 1839, that 'in consequence of the lamentable failure of most of our modern chapels, I have come to the resolution to subscribe to no buildings which are not erected under the designs and superintendence of Mr Pugin'.[38] Pugin thereby secured commissions for further large churches at St Mary's, Derby (1837–9),[39] St George's Cathedral, Southwark (1840–8), where he was named as architect in 1838,[40] St Chad's Cathedral, Birmingham (1839–41), and St Barnabas' Cathedral, Nottingham (1842–4), at each of which Shrewsbury was merely one of the many benefactors, albeit the most generous. The Earl also made substantial benefactions to St Peter's College Chapel, Wexford (1839–41),[41] the new monastery and church at Mount St Bernard (1840–4), to Oscott College, Handsworth Mercy Convent (1840–1), and St Wilfrid's, Cotton (1846–8). To each Shrewsbury made the largest individual donation and also brought his architect Pugin. This approach however failed with the Jesuits. At the church of the Immaculate Conception which they were building at Farm Street, Mayfair, Shrewsbury's offer of £500 in 1842[42] did not persuade them to abandon their architect J. J. Scoles;[43] Fr Lythgoe complained: 'Mr Pugin is too expensive and will not allow competition'[44] (i.e. amongst builders). As a result Fr Lythgoe received the money only in 1845. Pugin later however designed the high altar at the behest of another donor and against the architect's wishes.[45] In addition to gifts for missions and for building, Lord Shrewsbury gave £1,000 a year to Dr Walsh.

Projects such as the cathedrals at Birmingham, Nottingham and even Southwark, although not entirely Shrewsbury's gifts, were unthinkable without his support, and with that support went the services of Pugin. The psychological effect of the Earl's generosity was more decisive than the actual amount given. His greatest contribution to the Catholic Revival was as the patron and supporter of Pugin, Walsh and Wiseman when their projects seemed merely fantastic.

HARDMAN & CO. AND THE HARDMAN FAMILY

One of A. W. Pugin's first contacts with the West Midlands was through the Hardman family of Handsworth, headed by John Hardman senior (1767–1844), the 'opulent button maker and medallist'.[46] It was to Hardman that Pugin sent his first scheme to rebuild the modest St Chad's chapel, Birmingham, the forerunner of the cathedral scheme.[47] Hardman was the donor of many objects to Pugin's actual cathedral, notably the rood screen;[48] here his family was to be buried in the Hardman chantry, given to the family in recognition of their charities in 1844.[49] His son John Hardman junior (1812–1867),[50] collaborated with Pugin over the expansion of the metalwork business into church furniture and, from 1845, stained glass. His nephew, John Hardman Powell (1827–1894) who married Pugin's eldest daughter Anne in 1850, claimed to be Pugin's only pupil, and took over the glass design aspect on Pugin's death in 1852.[51] He attempted to collaborate with E. W. Pugin, first seen in the design of the funeral arrangements of the Earl of Shrewsbury in November 1852,[52] and to continue the second generation of the Pugin-Hardman collaboration. After E. W. Pugin's death in 1875 this was continued by the Pugin & Pugin firm. For three generations this was an essential ingredient of their successful domination of church architecture and decoration, and of their influence in the Catholic Revival in the Midlands.[53]

AMBROSE PHILLIPPS DE LISLE

Another lay collaborator of Pugin's, 'a Christian after his own heart',[54] was the Leicestershire squire Ambrose Phillipps; he added de Lisle (the name of his mother's ancestors) on inheriting from his father in 1862. While still a school boy he was received into the Church in 1824 and then practised his faith as an undergraduate at Trinity College, Cambridge, marrying into the Catholic Clifford family in 1833. He lived at Grace Dieu Manor, and by 1837 was supporting a Catholic mission there and at two other sites on the estate.[55] He began the first Cistercian monastery in England since the Reformation, and encouraged the Rosminians to come to Leicestershire. Like Pugin he made early and sincere attempts to contact the Oxford Movement, visiting Oxford in April 1841, and providing at Grace Dieu a meeting place for the suspicious protagonists on both the Anglican and Catholic sides.[56] Phillipps's patrimony was too small for his piety, and much of it was spent in expectation of inheritances (from his father and from the Earl of Shrewsbury) which did not materialize. The costs of the Catholic projects associated with him were largely borrowed from or paid for by others, the monastery of Mount St Bernard and the Shepshed church, for example, by Lord Shrewsbury and Bishop Walsh. Grace Dieu was given up before Phillipps's death, and the family debts on the monastery were repaid only in 1899.

BISHOP WALSH

Bishop Thomas Walsh (1776–1849), Vicar Apostolic of the Midland District 1826–40 and of the new Central District 1840–7, was recognized by many as the leading Catholic bishop.[57] He was in Pugin's view 'the only Bishop in England who has really advanced the dignity of religion. Dr Walsh found the churches in his district worse than barns; he will leave them sumptuous erections.'[58] For Walsh he began St Chad's Cathedral in 1839, the first Catholic church to be planned as a cathedral since the Reformation. Here Walsh, who died as Vicar Apostolic of the London District in 1849, was to be buried under an elaborate wall monument designed by Pugin and made by George Myers's craftsmen. It was shown at the Great Exhibition in 1851 and commented on by Queen Victoria, who asked 'who the monumental tomb was of – and asked who Dr Walsh was'.[59] His most important role was perhaps as President of Oscott College.

THE ROLE OF OSCOTT COLLEGE

Pugin's most significant Catholic patronage links were made in 1837. They began with his first visit to Oscott in March, where in April he met Bishop Walsh and Fr Spencer; by June he was refurnishing the chapel and in August making an architectural tour with the President, Dr Henry Weedall.[60] On 29 May he met John Hardman senior, to whom he sent twelve days later a complete new church scheme for the St Chad's chapel.[61] In October he met Thomas Griffiths, the Vicar Apostolic of the London District, and following a round of clerical dinners he had secured the commission for St George's, Southwark, by January 1838.[62] In November he met Ambrose Phillipps at Grace Dieu Manor, and fell on his neck, exclaiming that he had found a Christian after his own heart.[63] In between these meetings and visits Pugin began work at St Mary's College Oscott, or as he preferred for dedications to the Blessed Virgin, 'St Marie's', another piece of neo-mediaevalism; the pronunciation is 'Mary', not a frenchified 'Marie' with which it is sometimes confused. In November he delivered his first lecture to the seminarians at Oscott, describing himself as 'Professor of Ecclesiastical Antiquities', and began to refurnish the public rooms of the College and create the Museum.[64] It was under this professorial title that he published some of his most important architectural theories, including his *True Principles of Pointed or Christian Architecture set forth in two lectures delivered at St Marie's, Oscott* (1841).

The building of the new seminary at Oscott by the architect Joseph Potter[65] was the most ambitious Catholic architectural scheme then in progress in England. Pugin dramatically took over from him the furnishing of the new seminary and its chapel. He is popularly supposed to have added the five-sided apse to the chapel, but this was an alteration by Potter. Pugin's first appearance at Oscott was not as architect but as antique dealer and furniture designer, an earlier career role. Through his connection with the London antique trade, he procured the medieval and baroque fittings that made the chapel so exceptional. His furnishing bills survive for 1838 and 1839, and they establish his refurnishing at Oscott as his most important commission since his early involvement at Windsor Castle.[66] The chapel was furnished with antiques procured by Pugin, the most notable being the fifteenth-century Flemish reredos (reassembled with nineteenth-century additions in its present form).[67] There is circumstantial evidence that behind the lavishness of Oscott was the fortune of the Venerable Ignatius Spencer, the convert son of the second Earl Spencer and the first Catholic to visit the Tractarians in Oxford.[68] There were also benefactions both in cash and kind by Lord Shrewsbury who presented many paintings and vestments.[69]

At Oscott College chapel the appointments of the private country house chapel (as at Alton Towers) were brought for the first time to the public worship of the Church and the formation of the clergy. Pugin himself designed and donated metalwork for the altar (the high altar candlesticks are inscribed as his *ex voto* gift) and silver plate for the Mass and for the bishop's offices.

At the consecration of Oscott chapel in May 1838 Pugin dominated this strictly liturgical, and therefore clerical, ceremony to the astonishment of contemporaries. He was as prominent as the consecrating bishops themselves, usurping clerical roles within the sanctuary itself. There was hostile comment on the impropriety of such a liturgical role for a recent convert, and one who was moreover a married man; this role earned him the sobriquet 'Archbishop Pugens'.[70] The ceremonies were widely reported in the Catholic press, with Pugin's role prominently underlined. Ullathorne recalled: 'Pugin, with his eyes flashing through his tears, was in raptures, declaring it the first great day for England since the Reformation.'[71] The clergy meekly gave up their lighter and more comfortable 'French' vestments at Pugin's insistence. He introduced for the first time the fuller cut gothic cloth of gold High Mass vestments, which he himself designed and which were made by Tyler & Lonsdale, the gift of Lord Shrewsbury. The Oscott chapel was intended to raise liturgical standards in the formation of the clerical students; it had stalls arranged choir-wise, the clerical students and boys being seated on benches in the body of the nave, and the public relegated to ante-chapels. The present choir arrangement with seating entirely in stalls dates from 1925, as a comparison of historic photographs makes clear.[72]

THE ROLE OF ST CHAD'S CATHEDRAL

Since 1833 Bishop Walsh had been considering the building of a cathedral and seems to have taken considerable interest in church building even before Pugin's arrival at Oscott. The Bishop and his clergy discussed plans for new churches at their annual meeting. The projects, however, were modest for so vast a vicariate, stretching from Wales to East Anglia. In 1832 only three new chapels were opened, typically financed not by the Bishop but by private donors.[73] In 1833 Walsh made the ambitious suggestion of regularized and centralized collections instead of the haphazard, local collections begun for church building. The Birmingham cathedral, however, implied the merger of the two extant Birmingham congregations so as to found a larger church as 'a Cathedral worthy of the metropolis of the whole district'.[74] But centralized collections or attempts to direct the clergy or policy of existing missions were beyond the administrative powers of the vicars apostolic and most bishops even after 1850. Walsh's plans were hotly resisted by Thomas McDonnell of St Peter's, Birmingham, and the proposed cathedral languished amid clerical and congregational factionalism.[75] The local architect Thomas Rickman[76] and the Catholic Joseph Aloysius Hansom were both asked to produce designs, but they were supplanted by Pugin who in the space of ten days designed a new chapel (as even he called it in his diary) to replace the existing St Chad's chapel.[77] With Shrewsbury's and Pugin's support the Bishop's project became a reality, sidestepping the 'congregationalism' of the two rival Birmingham Catholic congregations.

At St Chad's the departure from usual 'congregational' church-building practice was recorded in two separate statements. The first was a disclaimer, inscribed on a neo-medieval illuminated parchment signed by John Hardman and others, of their 'congregational' proprietary rights over the new building: 'We, the Catholics of Birmingham ... do, by these presents, make a free and voluntary surrender of all that we have hitherto given towards the erection and advancement of the cathedral.'[78] The second claimed that 'Bishop Walsh ... of his own free-will determined, without consulting any committee or human counsel, resolved to commence at once a noble gothic cathedral ...'[79] Until the 1830s such patronage had provided for church building in towns organized by lay committees, which built a specific church or managed the entire temporalities of the mission. Pugin, with his romantic view of the pious church-building bishops – 'a Wykeham in every Bishop'[80] – and of generous seigneurs such as Shrewsbury, was deeply hostile to this oligarchic, quasi-nonconformist organization. Pugin associated lay committees with his other bêtes noires of hired seats and orchestral church openings: 'I am a stranger to fear; and all the fiddlers, and organists, and performers and committee men in England would not prevent me ...'[81] His impact on corporate, lay-directed 'congregational' church building was one of the most dramatic of his interventions.

In fact the whole 'congregational' structure broke down under the weight of responsibility, which churches such as Pugin's now implied.[82] His meeting with a committee at Southwark in 1839 led to his resignation as he 'collected his plans . . . rolled them up, took his hat, wished the gentlemen good day, and walked out of the house, leaving the Committee in perfect astonishment at his inexplicable conduct'. Pugin explained later that 'I . . . supposed that I was dealing with people who knew what they wanted. The absurd questions, however, showed my mistake.'[83] The committee resigned immediately after him. In the event large churches at Southwark and Clayton Street, Newcastle (1842-4),[84] were not the product of 'congregational' committees but of the combination of an ambitious architect, dedicated clergy, generous individual donors and, above all, a willingness to shoulder debt.

At St Chad's, with twelve months' experience of church building and the collaboration of his new builder George Myers, Pugin's 1839 scheme was markedly more practical than his church designs even of 1837. Pugin's drawings and Myers's estimates – a formality which they dispensed with later as their collaboration prospered – gave Walsh the practical data for the building of a large church previously unavailable.[85] The cathedral was built astonishingly quickly; started in 1839, it was consecrated in 1841 with its full complement of ritual and decorative furnishings. Pugin was also now able to rely on the partnership built up since 1838 with John Hardman senior and junior, whose craftsmen were responsible for metalwork and other furnishings. For both Pugin and the Hardmans the roles of designer and donor were of course interdependent, and Pugin threatened to resign the commission when the rood screen – a feature obviously suggested by Pugin – was threatened by Wiseman in 1840.[86] Shrewsbury gave £1,000 in 1839 and fittings in 1841. Hardman senior gave £250 and his son £50 at the foundation, with other many furnishings including the rood screen by the time of the opening. In 1844 John Hardman junior privately estimated the contract cost at £12,000, the furnishings at £8,000.[87] The Bishop, who had £2,000 to contribute, later came into a £12,000 legacy.[88] Pugin was to combine the role of both architect and 'sacristan' in the sense of liturgist or master of ceremonies for the consecration of St Chad's. The liturgical ceremonies lasted for five days and included a public fast, the translation of the recently rediscovered relics of St Chad to the new church, the consecration of the church and of the side altars, and, on the fifth day, the opening.[89] Pugin, who often complained of the use to which churches were put, spoke of the office of the sacristan in the management of the liturgy and furnishings of a church as perhaps even more important than that of the architect himself; hence his assumption of both roles. Pugin's name was associated with that of the Earl of Shrewsbury himself at the dinner to mark the blessing of the foundation, when he even regaled the diners with another architectural lecture occupying four pages of published text.[90] Thereafter Pugin claimed that the splendour of the liturgies at St Chad's, where the Gregorian chant was used, encouraged its further decoration: 'see Birmingham is cramed [*sic*] full every sunday eving [*sic*] ailes [*sic*] standing room & all.'[91] The cathedral was a magnet for those fascinated by the Gothic Revival: the schoolboy St George Mivart was prevented only by the family servant travelling with him from being received after attending a High Mass.[92]

THE OPENING OF ST GILES, CHEADLE, 1846

Pugin had predicted of St Giles that 'all the learned men will flock to this church as a model'.[93] Its opening on 1 September 1846 was eagerly anticipated, as the mounting excitement in the flurry of the metalwork orders from Hardman & Co. in June, July and August shows, of which the single most expensive item was the brass screen to the Blessed Sacrament chapel, costing £251 14s.[94] Cheadle, unlike many of Pugin's other commissions, is so complete, so satisfying and so rich, that a visit to this church alone proves his importance in the

Catholic Revival both in England and Europe. He was right to call it 'Cheadle. *Perfect* Cheadle, Cheadle my consolation in all afflictions'.[95] Amongst the clergy, the newly received Newman, shortly to be associated with Pugin's critics, described the Blessed Sacrament chapel as 'a blaze of light – and I could not help saying to myself "*Porta Coeli*"'.[96]

St Giles is of unique importance in nineteenth-century Catholic church-building, and was widely influential too on Anglicans and on European Catholic visitors. The leaders of the Catholic and the Gothic Revivals on the Continent were invited to the opening, including the Catholic politician the Comte de Montalembert,[97] the publisher Adolphe-Napoléon Didron[98] and the stained glass artist Henri Gérente[99] from France, as well as August Richensperger,[100] the Catholic politican behind the completion of Cologne Cathedral. Pugin's prominence and his role in the ceremony struck visitors from Catholic countries as unusual. A. N. Didron, describing them as 'pèlerins d'archéologie, comme autrefois pèlerins de piété'. He contrasted the situation at church openings in France where 'l'architecte n'existait pas; il se cachait avec sa jeune femme dans un coin de la nef.'[101]

The influence of St Giles in England was assured through Pugin's many church-building imitators, both Catholic and Protestant; the prolific George Gilbert Scott (later architect of the Albert Memorial, who included Pugin amongst the architects depicted on its plinth) was one visitor,[102] and the most plagiarist imitator was the architect Henry Woodyer's church of Holy Innocents (1849–51) at Highnam, Gloucestershire.[103] For foreigners the most striking aspect was perhaps what continental critics called a *Gesamtkunstwerk* or complete artwork, that is an example of the applied arts as the product of one controlling mind, as Wagner's operas were to be. Pugin's hand was in all the profusion of stonework, metalwork, woodwork, ceramics, stained glass, textiles, paintwork, gilding.[104] It inspired Baron Jean-Baptiste Béthune at St Mary Magdalene, Vivenkapelle near Bruges, and later the Guilde de Saint-Thomas et de Saint-Luc which he founded.[105] Didron's initial enthusiastic accounts of Pugin's 'resurrection of the

Middle Ages, body and soul' had been revised by the time of Pugin's death in 1852.[106] Pugin boldly set out to re-create the full repertoire of the English medieval parish church of the year 1300, and such was his success that contemporary historians of the English Decorated style point to the authenticity of its use of decoration and colour.[107] That Pugin could do so is a testament to his own authority as an antiquarian (evidenced by his position at Oscott) and his brilliance as a designer of decoration and detail.

The lavish cost and liturgical programme of Cheadle is something of a comment on the impractically narrow base of Pugin's 'English' Catholic programme. The iconographic badges of priest, deacon, and sub-deacon on the sedilia in the sanctuary display the ritual organization of the English medieval Sarum rite, not the then current Tridentine rite, in which the Easter sepulchre arrangement was also totally redundant. What was the purpose of such churches for poverty stricken, working-class congregations that surely had more need of schools and Mercy Sisters than plain chant and High Masses? Few Catholic congregations had a Lord Shrewsbury ready to make such a grand seigneural gesture, and these churches were often built (as here) at the whim of a Catholic magnate or more likely a Catholic convert, and often far from centres of population where the clergy struggled alone. The vicissitudes and struggles of the clergy at Cheadle make an interesting contrast to the undeniable architectural claims of the church. Biographies of the priests make one realize not only how heroic but also how tenuous the whole project was, particularly after the deaths of the 16th and 17th Earls of Shrewsbury. Canon Paul Jones sold his books and his piano to make ends meet and died 'in great poverty and in a state of near starvation' in 1860, to be succeeded by priests who stayed one, ten and three years respectively. One of the curates is said to have been 'at times a bit queer owing to his having received a severe bang on the head during the Murphy Riots', which took place in Birmingham in 1867. And there was friction between the English Catholics and their Irish priests such as William Gubbins (priest here 1847–55). By

1874 the congregation was reduced to twenty, but the next priest, appointed in 1874, was here for a patriarchal span of sixty years.[108]

PUGIN AND THE CLERGY

The sobriquet 'Archbishop Pugens' reminds us of the reactions which Pugin provoked. He had sharp words for the clergy who misunderstood his programme, denouncing the use of his church at Dudley: 'the churches I build do little or no good for want of men who know how to use them ... The church at Dudley is a compleat [*sic*] facsimile of one of the old English parish churches and nobody seems to know how to use it.'[109] This was a surprising claim since the patron was George Spencer, who had commissioned the church from Pugin in 1838, built to a different scheme in 1839–40. In the Midlands Pugin generally found many influential clergy sympathetic to his programme, such as Dr Weedall (who in 1846 actually managed to erect a rood screen in the chapel at Oscott), and Dr John Moore at St Chad's.[110] Another was Robert William Willson at Nottingham who was closely associated with the building of St Barnabas' Cathedral, and who, on appointment as bishop for the new diocese of Hobart, Tasmania, in 1842, took with him Pugin vestments, metalwork, stained glass and even demountable wooden models of churches as exemplars.[111]

Pugin's most problematic relationship was with Nicholas Wiseman, who arrived at Oscott in 1840 as co-adjutor bishop to Walsh. While still Rector of the English College in Rome, Wiseman seems to have been ready to commission an Italian (or perhaps Latin) edition of *Contrasts*,[112] and he translated for a Roman congregation a letter describing Pugin's churches, referring to him as 'insigne architteto Sig. Pugin convertito alla fede cattolica'.[113] But Pugin had violent disagreements with Wiseman as President of Oscott, especially over the rood screen at St Chad's, expressing his disappointment to Dr Rock and other correspondents.[114] Pugin's misunderstanding of the force of Wiseman's Roman ethos is shown by his naïve claim to an Anglican correspondent that in his Easter 1842 liturgies at St Chad's 'Dr Wiseman is now compleatly *ad usum sarum*',[115] imagining him to have abandoned his Roman liturgical preferences for Pugin's neo-medievalism, that is adopting the pre-1559 Sarum Rite.

In August 1844, at the opening of St Barnabas' Cathedral, Nottingham, Wiseman publicly eulogized Pugin as the architect of over thirty Catholic churches.[116] He was not to be praised by bishops from the pulpits again, at least before his funeral. Wiseman's next great cathedral opening, St George's, Southwark, in July 1848, was to mark the beginning of the Rood Screen Controversy. A different example was that of W. B. Ullathorne, Vicar Apostolic of the Central District from 1848 and Bishop of Birmingham from 1850 who, although he had known of Pugin's leading role in 1838, treated C. F. Hansom[117] who had designed for him the church of the Most Holy Sacrament and St Osburg, Coventry, as 'his' architect.[118]

Pugin built few new churches after the opening of Cheadle, an event which Wiseman did not attend. Instead he was at the opening of Hansom's Our Blessed Lady and St Alphonsus, Blackmore Park, Worcestershire (1844–6), of which Ullathorne claimed a direct role in the design.[119] One of the most impressive churches in the new diocese, SS Thomas and Edmund of Canterbury, Erdington (1849–51), was also by Hansom.[120] Here the donor, the convert priest Daniel Haigh,[121] commissioned from Pugin not the church itself but its altar metalwork and glass instead.[122] Pugin was thus reduced to designing fittings and decoration for churches by others, losing the actual architectural commission. He was aware of the threat to his exclusive claims and lamented: 'There are so many Catholic architects now that there is no chance of any buildings. I believe I design for them all, for I actually see my own casts and figures used, and then they abuse me afterwards. These men can afford to sell cheap for they *steal* their *brooms ready* made.'[123] Hansom also supplanted Pugin with the Rosminians at Ratcliffe College, Leicestershire,[124] and at Rugby.[125] Ullathorne, Wiseman and others were all moving away from an early association with Pugin, while some, even Wiseman, began to associate Pugin's Gothic Revival with their earlier flirtation with the Oxford Movement.

PUGIN AND THE OXFORD MOVEMENT

Pugin had been one of the first Catholics to make contact with figures in the Oxford Movement in the Anglican Church, active since 1833 in defending the independence of the state church against the interference of Parliament. Its leaders, especially Newman, carefully eschewed all contact with English and especially Irish Catholics. However, in 1839 Pugin met the Revd John Bloxam of Magdalen College, Oxford,[126] and in October 1840 W. G. Ward and others.[127] Pugin and the few Catholics subscribing to his 'English' Catholic model, were very sympathetic to the 'Oxford men', of whom he wrote to Lord Shrewsbury: 'These men will Catholicise England.'[128] By 1841 Cambridge enthusiasts such as the Revd Benjamin Webb, founder of the Cambridge Camden Society (1839), were also approaching Pugin on the basis of shared antiquarian and architectural enthusiasms. His relationship with the Cambridge Movement and its magazine *The Ecclesiologist* (1841–68), which largely recycled Pugin's teachings for an Anglican audience, was to prove to be unhappy.[129] A more tangible outcome of these contacts was Pugin's commissions to build the gateway at Magdalen College, Oxford (1844),[130] and a small Anglican village church of St Lawrence (1847) at Tubney, Oxfordshire, largely at Bloxam's behest.[131] Pugin church-building in the University cities was confined to the small Catholic church of St Andrew, Union St, Cambridge (1841–3). Although there is a mention of an 'Oxford church' in his diary in 1840,[132] this was never realized: despite petitions and even a letter from Wiseman, the Jesuits would not act, and their diminutive classical chapel on St Clement's Lane[133] coninued as the physical expression of Catholicism in Oxford.

Oxford itself was also the scene of Pugin's great humiliation over the rejection of his scheme to rebuild Balliol

College, but given the sectarian temper of the time it was perhaps unlikely that the Anglican clergy who comprised the dons of Oxford would allow in a Trojan horse like Pugin.[134] While a handful of visionaries on both sides, even for a time Wiseman, expected a reunion between the two Churches, neither side could deliver the rest of their constituency, yet alone their full Church.[135] Newman's long-pondered decision to become a Catholic in 1845 threw the Oxford Movement onto the defensive and confirmed both Anglican suspicions and the Roman Catholic preference for the conversion of individuals as the only way to proceed.

THE END OF THE 'ENGLISH' CATHOLIC CHURCH?

Between Wiseman's private reflections on Alton Towers in 1835, his interest in *Contrasts* and his praise of Pugin at the opening of St Barnabas' Cathedral in 1844, and the attacks on Pugin following the opening of St George's, Southwark, a whole new clerical ethos had arisen. Pugin, who had been an initial intermediary, was to clash with Oxford Movement figures who had now became Catholics, notably Newman and W. G. Ward, in the Rood Screen Controversy.[136] This broke out in 1848 with Pugin's confrontation with Frederick Faber at Cotton, and quickly involved Phillipps and Shrewsbury on one side and Newman on the other. Pugin's opponents even identified him with a whole '-ism', speaking of 'Puginism'[137] as the check on the ultramontane and Italianizing style which they now preferred, as typified by the newly formed London Oratory.[138] By 1851 a hostile commentator was to say that 'we have ever associated Puginism with Puseyism,'[139] a reference to those who under the leadership of Dr Pusey broke with Newman.

Pugin's impact on Catholic architectural patronage in the 1830s and 1840s was similar to that elsewhere in his secular career, that is immediate success, then stagnation and decline. Ten years after the consecration of Oscott, Pugin was to find himself excluded from church-building in the Midlands and in London. While Shrewsbury's patronage never failed him, the early connections with Bishop Wiseman did not survive. Shrewsbury himself built no important church after the opening of St Giles, Cheadle, in 1846. Shrewsbury's opinions were initially sought by the bishops and by Rome, but his influence, like that of Pugin, was to be questioned in the later 1840s. He had no voice in the appointment of the new bishops in 1850, but with a diocese named after his title came the generous offer to build a cathedral at Shrewsbury, actually carried out by his heir and Pugin's son E. W. Pugin.[140]

THE DEATH OF THE EARL OF SHREWSBURY

The 'English' Catholic Church project had been largely financed by the Earl of Shrewsbury, although his benefactions were wildly exaggerated in the eulogy at his funeral, when it was claimed that he had spent over half a million pounds a year on church building.[141] But like the later benefactions of the 14th and 15th Dukes of Norfolk, Lord Shrewsbury's can be seen as an attempt to maintain his influence within the Church. Although he felt called upon to defend publicly the Restoration of the Hierarchy in 1850, in his *Letter to the Rt. Hon. the Lord John Russell* (1851),[142] he was ambivalent about it and temperamentally opposed to the clerical resurgence that it implied; rather he viewed the clergy as his chaplains.[143] No matter how individually compliant, as a body the clergy were engaged in freeing themselves from precisely the lay domination which Shrewsbury represented. George Montgomery, an Anglo-Irish convert priest in the Midlands, the scene of Shrewsbury's greatest benefactions, expressed in 1857 a view perhaps current even before the Earl's death: 'I am not one who would join in the cry to any earthly patron, "Oculi omnium in te sperant, domine", as we seemed lately to cry to Lord Shrewsbury; but I do not despise the aid of the worldly great, and would do what I could without flunkeyism to secure it.'[144]

Pugin died on 14 September 1852 and his funeral took place in the presence of only two bishops but many priests.[145] The

Earl of Shrewsbury died unexpectedly in Naples on 9 November 1852. His body was brought to England to an elaborate liturgical reception at St George's Cathedral. His requiems, which were held over thirty days, took place in the Talbot Gallery at Alton Towers as the chapel itself was fitted out for one of the most elaborate liturgical *coups de théâtre* such as Pugin had loved to orchestrate. Blacked out and candle-lit, the chapel was dominated by the torch-lit *chapelle ardente* within which the coffin was placed on a bier, all designed by E. W. Pugin and made by Hardman, at a cost of over £2,000. On the morning of 14 December, Masses were said continuously from 6 a.m. until the High Mass was begun in the presence of four bishops, many religious and over one hundred and fifty priests. The Earl was then buried under the simple brass at St John's, Alton.[146] Of Lord Shrewsbury's contribution to the Catholic Revival it must be said: 'Quantitative judgements don't apply.'[147]

E. W. PUGIN

The role of Shrewsbury and Pugin in the Midlands was to devolve on the unsure shoulders of the twenty-year-old Bertram Talbot (1832–1856), who succeeded as 17th Earl of Shrewsbury[148] and the eighteen-year-old Edward Welby Pugin. The new Earl, second cousin of the 16th Earl, continued the commitments to certain churches and gave £500 a year to the Birmingham diocese. Edward Welby Pugin (1834–1875) was already describing himself as an architect before his father's death and he naturally succeeded to his father's practice.[149] He had a strong claim to be called his father's pupil and he initially continued Pugin's 'archaeological' reliance on the fourteenth-century English Decorated style, of which the best example is Oulton Abbey in Staffordshire, a commission inherited from his father,[150] but he was to develop quite differently after 1856. His buildings are characterized by their contrasting building materials and polychromatic effects, by their attenuated proportions and height, and their massive roof structures. The most instructive comparison between the two is St Marie, Rugby (1864), where his father's church of 1847 became a side chapel; the fine interior survives.[151] Another contrast with his father's work is at St Joseph, Nechells, Birmingham, built by A. W. Pugin in 1850 as the chapel to the projected Birmingham Catholic cemetery where Edward added two naves and the priest's house in 1872.[152]

Edward's designs were much busier than his father's. His delight in elaborate architectural and figure carving can be seen in the beautiful altar now at Henley-on-Thames, an elaboration of his father's work in the nearby private chapel at Danesfield.[153] Edward also made a significant contribution to the development of Hardman & Co., particularly in metalwork and stained glass, often in collaboration with his brother-in-law John Hardman Powell.[154] He built several important new churches in the diocese, although his best, Longton (1868–9), where the future Bishop Edward Isley was curate, was demolished in 1970.[155] Other notable buildings include St Austin, Stafford (1862)[156] and Our Lady and All Saints, Stourbridge (1864).[157] He built schools and convents, and proposed major additions to Cotton College in 1866.[158] The plan of the cheap, brick church at Warwick (1860) is related to the church of Our Lady, Eldon Street, Liverpool, a highly influential church which, it was claimed, reconciled the clergy to the Gothic and solved the problems of the Rood Screen Controversy, marking 'a complete revolution in church-building' as the *Tablet* put it.[159]

The implicit claim of E. W. Pugin to be successor to his father's role was not to be accepted by Bishop Ullathorne, under whose leadership churches were much less ambitious; after 1856 he effectively forbade church building without his specific financial approval.[160] E. W. Pugin got himself into a major misunderstanding with Ullathorne over his 1866 scheme for Cotton and by 1874 was denouncing the bishop and his vicar general as his 'enemies' over this and the loss of the commission for St Catherine, Horsefair, Birmingham, to A. M. Dunn.[161] Ullathorne at first favoured C. F. Hansom, and then A. M. Dunn and E. J. Hansom (perhaps suggested by their rebuilding of Downside monastery and the new abbey church),[162] for churches, and for his pet project of the St Bernard's Seminary, Olton.[163] Thereafter he was more involved with religious orders as patrons, especially the Benedictines,[164] notably at Belmont Abbey[165] and in the close collaboration with the Ampleforth monk Laurence Shepherd, the chaplain at Stanbrook Abbey, where the new chapel and its furnishings was one of the most important of his career.[166] New churches for the missions were no longer the primary commissions: E. W. Pugin's drawings of 1865 for a new church at Sutton Coldfield remained only on paper, perhaps because the bishop would not agree its financing.[167] The heroic church building of the days of Pugin and Shrewsbury had been firmly curtailed by the new hierarchy.

Notes

1. Ferrey, *Recollections*, p. 86.
2. *Catholic Magazine*, III (1839), p. 498; B. Ward, *The Sequel to Catholic Emancipation* (1915), I, pp. 119–21.
3. *Tablet* (1844), p. 580.
4. Ferrey, *Recollections*, p. 88; The 'good chapel' is thought to be that at Stonyhurst, by J. J. Scoles: M. Trappes Lomax, *Pugin, a Mediaeval Victorian* (1932).
5. Thomas Rickman (1776–1841) was a Unitarian.
6. Hansom was in partnership with E. Welch: R. O'Donnell, 'The Hansom family', in J. Turner (ed.), *The Grove Dictionary of Art*, XVI (London and New York, 1996), p. 156.
7. Blore MS, Cambridge University Library, ADD MS 8170/84, Spencer to Blore, 3 March 1835.
8. P. Stanton, *Pugin* (1971); R. O'Donnell, 'Pugin as a Church Architect', in P. Atterbury and C. Wainwright (eds), *Pugin: A Gothic Passion* (New Haven and London, 1994), pp. 63–89; A. Wedgwood, 'A. W. N. Pugin', in Turner (ed.), *The Grove Dictionary of Art*, XXV, pp. 711–16.
9. *OJ*, IX (1839), 33–6, 187–8.
10. Ibid., VIII (1839), 105–6.
11. Notably by Wiseman, *Dublin Review*, 3 (1837), pp. 360–84;

R. Hill, 'Reformation to Millennium: Pugin's *Contrasts* in the History of English Thought', in *Journal of the Society of Architectural Historians* (USA), 58 (1999), 26–41.

12. Below, gazetteer.
13. *OJ*, IX (1839), 270–2; Ward, *Sequel*, I, pp. 114–16.
14. Ward, *Sequel*, I, pp. 114–18; E. S. Purcell, *Life and Letters of Ambrose Phillipps de Lisle*, II (1900), pp. 219–24.
15. R. E. Guy, *The Synods in English* (Stratford-upon-Avon, 1886), p. 42. The ban was unsuccessful.
16. *OJ*, IX (1839), 129–32. The architect, Charles Day, was a Catholic.
17. *OJ*, IX (1839), 396–8; *Catholic Magazine*, III (1839), 342.
18. Pugin, 'Lectures on ecclesiastical architecture ... lecture the second', in *Catholic Magazine*, II (June 1838) p. 332. For Moorfields see R. O'Donnell, 'The interior of St Mary, Moor-fields', in *The Georgian Group Journal*, VII (1997), 71–4.
19. M. Belcher (ed.), *The Collected Letters of A. W. N. Pugin*, I (Oxford, 2001), p. 384.
20. *Dublin Review* (1839), p. 244.
21. H.-R. Hitchcock, *Early Victorian Architecture*, I (1951), p. 74.
22. B. Ward, *The Life and Times of Cardinal Wiseman* (1897) I, p. 215.
23. Omitted from the first edition of the *Dictionary of National Biography*; but see C. S. Nicholl (ed.), *Dictionary of National Biography: Missing Persons* (1993), pp. 661–2. He still lacks a biographer.
24. Pugin's Diary, 30 October 1837, in Wedgwood, *Pugin Family*, pp. 38 (note 55), 79.
25. Daniel Rock, FSA (1799–1871), Shrewsbury's chaplain 1827–40.
26. Pugin's Diary, 5 September 1836, in Wedgwood, *Pugin Family*, p. 36, note 31. Ferrey, *Recollections*, p. 117, locates the first meeting with Shrewsbury to the shop of Edward Hull, the Wardour Street antique dealer.
27. Ward, *Wiseman*, I, p. 215.
28. Pugin's Diary, 29–31 July 1840, in Wedgwood, *Pugin Family* pp. 46 (note 17), 84; *OJ*, XI (1840), 110–12; M. J. Fisher, *Alton Towers: A Gothic Wonderland* (Stafford, 1999), pp. 92–5.
29. Pugin's Diary, 2 January 1839, in Wedgwood, *Pugin Family*, p. 81, note 2. J. H. Talbot (1794–1868) was of Talbot Hall,

New Ross, Co. Wexford; his cousin Maria-Theresa married the 16th Earl.

30. Purcell, *Phillipps*, I, p. 80.
31. *Catholic Magazine and Review*, V (1834), 316.
32. Ibid., p. 664. The present church is by Albert Vicars, architect.
33. Pugin was supplying furniture for this church by 1838: Pugin's Diary, 15 September 1838, in Wedgwood, *Pugin Family*, pp. 40 (note 33), 81.
34. *Catholic Magazine and Review*, V (1834), pp. 662–3.
35. Belcher (ed.), *Letters of Pugin*, p. 270.
36. Ibid., p. 306.
37. *OJ*, VIII (1839), 15, 277–84.
38. S. J. Lander, 'Roman Catholicism', in *Victoria County History of Cheshire*, II, p. 93.
39. *OJ*, VII (1838), 37–8; VIII (1839), 385–7.
40. B. Bogan, *The Great Link: A History of St George's Cathedral, Southwark, 1786–1958* (1958).
41. R. O'Donnell, 'The Pugins in Ireland', in P. Atterbury (ed.), *A. W. N. Pugin: Master of the Gothic Revival* (New Haven and London, 1995), pp. 136–59.
42. Jesuit Archives, Farm Street, London, 'College of St Ignatius 1802–1865', f. 170, Shrewsbury to Fr Lythgoe, SJ, 1 January 1842.
43. John Joseph Scoles (1798–1863) was the favoured architect of the Jesuits, designing their churches at Stonyhurst, Preston, Liverpool and Yarmouth.
44. Ibid., f. 108, Lythgoe's refusal of Pugin, 10 August 1844, f. 205, Shrewsbury's payment, 17 July 1845.
45. B. Bassett, *Farm Street Church* (1948).
46. J. Gillow, *Bibliographical Dictionary of the English Catholics*, III, p. 128; W. Greaney, *A Guide to St Chad's Cathedral Church, Bath Street, Birmingham* (1877), pp. 24–6.
47. Below, p. 16.
48. Gillow, *Dictionary*, III, pp. 128–133.
49. The Cathedral Clergy, *A History of St Chad's Cathedral, Birmingham, 1841–1904* (Birmingham, 1904), pp. 153–4, and pp. 147–50 for list of burials.
50. Gillow, *Dictionary*, III, pp. 131–3; Greaney, *St Chad's*, pp. 43–4, 61; *A History of St Chad's Cathedral 1841–1904*, p. 153.
51. For his important memoir see A. Wedgwood (ed.), J. H.

Powell, 'Pugin in his home', *c.* 1884, *Architectural History*, (Journal of the Society of Architectural Historians, GB), 31 (1988), 171–201.

52. See R. O'Donnell, 'No "maimed rites": the funeral of the 16th Earl of Shrewsbury', in *True Principles: The Voice of the Pugin Society*, vol. 2, number four (Summer 2002), pp. 17–21.

53. There is no history of Hardman & Co., but see R. O'Donnell, 'Hardman Metalwork Folios from Birmingham', in *True Principles*, Summer 2001, pp. 7–9.

54. Purcell, *Phillipps*, II, p. 289.

55. *OJ*, V (1837), 282–5.

56. M. Pawley, *Faith and Family, The life and circle of Ambrose Phillipps de Lisle* (Norwich, 1994), p. 130.

57. He was President of Oscott 1818–26 and Vicar Apostolic of the London District 1847–9.

58. Pugin to Phillipps, 13 December 1839, in Belcher (ed.), *Letters of Pugin*, I, p. 127.

59. J. Crace to J. Hardman, quoted in A. Wedgwood, 'The Mediaeval Court', in Atterbury and Wainwright, *Pugin*, p. 239.

60. Pugin's Diary, 1837, in Wedgwood, *Pugin Family*, pp. 37–8 (notes), 77–80.

61. Pugin's Diary, 29 May, 10 June 1837, in Wedgwood, *Pugin Family* p. 37, note 33, 36 p. 78; BAA, B465, Pugin to Hardman, 10 June 1837 (printed in Belcher (ed.), *Letters of Pugin*, I, pp. 77–8).

62. *Catholic Magazine*, II (1838), 700; IV (1840), 825; R. O'Donnell, 'Pugin and Catholic London: an early divorce?' in *True Principles*, Winter 1988–9; Winter 1999–2000.

63. Purcell, *Phillipps*, II, p. 289.

64. W. Greaney, *Catalogue of Pictures, Wood-Carvings, Manuscripts and other Works of Art and Antiquities in St Mary's College, Oscott, 1880* (Birmingham, 1880).

65. Joseph Potter (*c.* 1756–1842) of Lichfield, was also part contractor with his sons Robert (*c.* 1795–1854) and Joseph (1792–1875) for the college: R. O'Donnell, 'Pugin at Oscott', in J. F. Champ (ed.), *Oscott College, 1838–1988, a volume of commemorative essays* (1988), pp. 48–9.

66. Ibid., pp. 50–4; O'Donnell, 'Pugin as a Church Architect', in Atterbury and Wainwright, *Pugin*, pp. 79–80.

67. A. Wedgwood, 'A. W. Pugin's Tours in Northern Europe', in

J. de Maeyer and L. Verpoest (eds), *Gothic Revival: Religion, Architecture and Style in Western Europe 1815–1914* (KADOC Artes, Leuven, 2000), pp. 92–4.

68. Purcell, *Phillipps*, I. p. 227; II, p. 214. J. H. Thomson, 'A History of Oscott College', IV, *The Oscotian*, NS, vol. 1 number 2 (1931), pp. 82–3.

69. Greaney, *Catalogue of Pictures . . . St Mary's College, Oscott, 1880.*

70. W. Buscot, *The History of Cotton College* (1940), p. 154.

71. W. B. Ullathorne, *From Cabin-boy to Archbishop*, ed. Shane Leslie (1941), p. 135.

72. Compare the photograph *c*. 1900, in J. F. Champ, *Oscott* (Archdiocese of Birmingham Historical Commission, 1987), p. 8, with that in C. Gallagher, *Oscott College: A Pictorial History* (Birmingham, 1994), p. 8.

73. *Catholic Magazine and Review*, III (1833), 484.

74. Ibid., IV (1833), pp. xxxiii–xxv.

75. For the Birmingham disputes see ibid. III–VI (1833–5) and J. F. Champ, 'Priesthood and Politics in the Nineteenth century: the turbulent career of Thomas McDonnell', in *Recusant History*, XVIII, 3 (1987), 289–303.

76. A design by Thomas Rickman dated 1831 is at the RIBA: J. Lever, *Catalogue of the Drawings Collection of the Royal Institute of British Architects*, vol. O–R, pp. 138–9.

77. Drawings signed by A. W. Pugin and dated 1837 for the 'Birmingham Catholic Church' are in BAA, APD/P1/1–6. See also Pugin's Diary, 10 June 1837, in Wedgwood, *Pugin Family*, p. 37, and note 36, p. 78.

78. Greaney, *St Chad's*, p. 36. The manuscript is in the sacristy at St Chad's Cathedral.

79. Ibid., p. 32. The phraseology is Greaney's.

80. Pugin, *Some Remarks on the Articles which have recently appeared in the 'Rambler'* . . . (1850), p. 18. William of Wykeham, Bishop of Winchester, was the builder of Winchester College and New College, Oxford.

81. *OJ*, IX (1839), 131.

82. For 'congregationalism' see J. Bossy, *English Catholic Community 1570–1850* (1975), pp. 295–363.

83. Ferrey, *Recollections*, p. 169.

84. R. O'Donnell, 'Pugin as a Church Architect', in Atterbury and Wainwright (eds), *Pugin*, pp. 68–9.

85. Pugin's contract drawings, signed by George Myers and Bishop Walsh, are at the RIBA: A. Wedgwood, *Catalogue of the Drawings Collection of the Royal Institute of British Architects, Pugin Family* (1977), pp. 55–6. His drawings for the Bishop's House are in BAA, APD/P1/7–11.

86. Pugin to Phillipps, 18 December 1840 [?], in Purcell, *Phillipps*, II, p. 213; Ward, *Sequel*, p. 17; Belcher (ed.), *Letters of Pugin*, I, pp. 174–6.

87. Birmingham City Archives, Hardman Collection, Letters 1839–98, 'bundle 1841–44', John Hardman to the Revd John Dalton.

88. For earlier estimates see *Catholic Magazine*, IV (1839), 42; for gifts by 1841: ibid., VI (1841), pp. 422–46; for later Shrewsbury and Hardman gifts: Greaney, *St. Chad's*, p. 35.

89. Ward, *Sequel*, II, pp. 12–15.

90. *Catholic Magazine*, IV (1841), 428–47.

91. Pugin to Shrewsbury, 24 December 1841, in Belcher (ed.), *Letters of Pugin*, I, pp. 306–8. For actual number of Birmingham Catholics see D. Mole, 'Challenge to the Church, Birmingham 1815–1865', in H. J. Dyos and M. Wolff (eds), *The Victorian City: Images and Realities*, II (1973), p. 821.

92. St George Mivart (1827–1900) became a Catholic on reaching his majority: obituary in *Tablet*, 7 April 1900. For his analysis of the period see 'The Conversion of England' IV, in *Dublin Review* (third series, XII, July–October 1884), pp. 65–86 (ref. supplied by the Revd Anthony Symondson, SJ).

93. Pugin to Shrewsbury, 19 March 1842, in Belcher (ed.), *Letters of Pugin*, I, p. 328.

94. Birmingham City Archives, Hardman Collection, Metalwork Daybook (1846–June 1848) 'no 74', June 16 1846, 'brass screen for the blessed sacrament ... four compartments set in low frame rich decorated brasswork, £25.14s; 2 mens' time (etc) £6.12s 6d., box and packing £3.2s 6d.'

95. Belcher (ed.), *Letters of Pugin*, I, p. 328.

96. J. H. Newman, *The Letters and Diaries of John Henry Newman* (ed. C. S. Dessain), XI, p. 210.

97. Charles-René Forbes de Tryon, Comte de Montalembert (1810–1870), French Catholic Liberal politican, whose *Du Vandalisme et du Catholicisme en l'Art* (1839) paralleled Pugin's *Contrasts*. He did not after all attend.

98. A. N. Didron *aîné* (1805?–1886), editor of the *Annales Archéologiques* (Paris).

99. Henri Gérente (1814–1849), the half-English stained glass artist whose business was continued after his death by his sculptor brother Alfred.

100. August Richensperger (1808–1895), editor of the *Kölner Domblatt*, later founder of the Catholic Centre Party; he visited Pugin at Ramsgate and wrote a memoir of him in 1877. See M. J. Lewis, *The Politics of the German Gothic Revival: August Richensperger* (Cambridge Massachusetts, 1993).

101. A. N. Didron, 'Promenade en Angleterre', in *Annales Archéologiques*, V (Paris, 1846), pp. 292–3. He also visited St John's Alton, and St Chad's.

102. G. Stamp, 'George Gilbert Scott, the Memorial Competition and its Critics', in C. Brooks (ed.) *The Albert Memorial, the Prince Consort National Memorial: its history, contexts, and conservation* (New Haven and London, 2000), pp. 112–14.

103. D. Verey, *Gloucestershire, the Vale and the Forest of Dean* (Harmondsworth, 1976), pp. 269–70.

104. R. O'Donnell, 'An Apology for the Revival: the architecture of the Catholic Revival in Britain and Ireland', in J. de Maeyer and L. Verpoest (eds), *Gothic Revival: Religion, Architecture and Style in Western Europe 1815–1914* (KADOC–Artes, Leuven, 2000), pp. 34–48.

105. Baron Jean-Baptist Béthune (1821–1894) was Pugin's most fervent European admirer and imitator, supremely in his church of O.-L.-Vroue.-Geboorte en H.-Fillipus Neri (1861–7), Vivenkapelle, near Bruges: J. de Maeyer, 'The Neo-Gothic in Belgium, Architecture for a Catholic Society', ibid., pp. 19–35.

106. *Annales Archéologiques*, XIII (1853), 335–7.

107. N. Coldstream, 'The Middle Pointed Revival, a mediaevalist's view', in F. Salmon (ed.), *The Gothic Revival*, papers from the 26th annual symposium of the Society of Architectural Historians (GB) (1997), pp. 17–24.

108. D. Higham and P. Carson, *Pugin's Churches of the Second Spring: An Historical Guide to the Catholic Churches of Cheadle, Alton and Cotton* (Uttoxeter, 1997), pp. 38–42.

109. Pugin to Phillipps, 18 December 1840, in Belcher (ed.), *Letters of Pugin*, I, pp. 174–6.

110. Canon John Moore, DD (1807–1856), professor (1832–40), then President (1848–53) of Oscott; missioner at St Chad's

(1840–8) and Handsworth (1853–6); said to have been the first to invite Pugin to Oscott in 1837 and to have introduced him to John Hardman: Dame Mary Francis Roskell, OSB, *Memoirs of Francis Kerrill Amherst, D.D.,* ed. H. Vaughan (1903), p. 193. Despite being Bishop Walsh's right-hand man, and expected successor, it was Bishop Ullathorne who succeeded in 1848.

111. Below, gazetteer; B. Andrews, 'Pugin in Australia', in Atterbury and Wainwright, *Pugin,* pp. 246–57; Andrews, *Creating a Gothic Paradise: Pugin at the Antipodes* (exhibition catalogue, Government of Tasmania and Hobart Archdiocese, 2002).

112. Pugin to Wiseman, 1 June and 20 August 1838, in Belcher (ed.), *Letters of Pugin,* I, pp. 82–5. Wiseman reviewed *Contrasts* in the *Dublin Review,* 3 (1837), pp. 360–84.

113. Wiseman's Italian draft, before 12 January 1840, in Belcher (ed.), *Letters of Pugin,* I, pp. 105–8.

114. Below, gazetteer, p. 59.

115. Belcher (ed.), *Letters of Pugin,* I, pp. 338–9.

116. *Tablet* (1844), p. 579.

117. C. F. Hansom (1816–1883) was the younger brother of Joseph Aloysius, architect of Birmingham Town Hall: R. O'Donnell, 'The Hansom family', in Turner (ed.), *The Grove Dictionary of Art,* XVI, p. 156.

118. C. Butler, *The Life and Times of Bishop Ullathorne* (1926), I, pp. 117–36; Dom Sebastian Simpson, OSB, *A Centenary Memorial of St Osburg's Coventry* (Coventry, 1945); Ullathorne, *Cabin-boy to Archbishop,* pp. 198–9, 211.

119. Ullathorne, *Cabin-boy,* p. 29. See also M. Hodgetts, *Blackmore Park 1596–1846–1996* (Upton-upon-Severn, 1996).

120. *Rambler* (1850), p. 90. There are many entries for Erdington in Birmingham City Archives, Hardman Collection, First Glass Day Book (No 34) 1845–50.

121. Daniel Henry Haigh (1819–1879) gave the lectern for Southwark Cathedral and episcopalia for Wiseman, including his mitre, all to Pugin's design: [R. O'Donnell] catalogue entry 56, in Atterbury (ed.), *Pugin, Master of the Gothic Revival.*

122. Ibid., catalogue entries 60, 63, 72.

123. Ferrey, *Recollections,* p. 133.

124. R. O'Donnell, 'Extra Illustrations of Pugin Buildings in T. H. King's "*Les Vrais Principes*"', in *Architectural History*

(Journal of the Society of Architectural Historians, GB), 44 (2001), pp. 57–63.

125. D. and L. Thackray, *A Brief History of St Marie's Church 1844–1986.*

126. Pugin's correspondence with Bloxam began 13 September 1840: Belcher (ed.), *Letters of Pugin*, I, pp. 142–7. For Pugin's visit to Exeter and Magdalen Colleges, see Diary 28–29 October 1840, in Wedgwood, *Pugin Family*, pp. 46 (notes 36, 37), 85.

127. W. G. Ward (1812–1882), then a Fellow of Balliol College, for whom Pugin later built a house at St Edmund's College, Ware: W. Ward, *W. G. Ward and the Catholic Revival* (1893), pp. 3, 386.

128. Belcher (ed.), *Letters of Pugin*, I, pp. 160–1, 187–9; Pawley, *Faith and Family*, pp. 112–13.

129. R. O'Donnell, '"Blink [him] by silence"?: the Cambridge Camden Society and A. W. N. Pugin', in C. Webster and J. Elliot (eds) *'A Church as it should be': The Cambridge Camden Society and its Influence* (Stamford, 2001), pp. 98–120.

130. R. White and R. Darwell-Smith, *The Architectural Drawings of Magdalen College, Oxford, a catalogue* (Oxford, 2001), pp. 120–4; the gateway was later demolished. Letters and a specification survive in the College archives. For his unexecuted scheme for the choir school, ibid., pp. 124–8. See also P. Spencer-Silver, *Pugin's Builder* (1993), p. 249.

131. Below, gazetteer.

132. Pugin's Diary, 11 May 1840, in Wedgwood, *Pugin Family*, pp. 45, 47, 84–5. The present writer thinks that the 'Oxford church' referred to is that at Radford.

133. Stanton, *Pugin*, p. 197; J. Bertram, *St Aloysius' Parish, Oxford* (Archdiocese of Birmingham Historical Commission, 1993), pp. 4–7.

134. H. M. Colvin, *Unbuilt Oxford* (1983), pp. 105–12.

135. P. B. Knockles, *The Oxford Movement in Context: Anglican High Churchmanship 1760–1857* (1994).

136. J. L. Altholz, *The Liberal Catholic Movement in England: the 'Rambler' and its Contributors, 1848–1864* (1960), pp. 14–16.

137. Newman's term in a letter to the editor of *The Rambler*, J. M. Capes, 18 February 1851: *Letters and Diaries* (ed. Dessain), XIV, pp. 213–15.

138. R. O'Donnell, 'The Architecture of the London Oratory Churches', in M. Napier and A. Laing (eds), *The London Oratory Centenary 1884–1984* (1984), pp. 21–47.
139. *Rambler*, VIII (1851), pp. 45–6.
140. J. Hall, *Shrewsbury Cathedral: A Sacrament in Stone* (Cathedral publication, 1994); R. O'Donnell, 'The Later Pugins', in Atterbury and Wainwright, *Pugin*, pp. 264–5.
141. Henry Weedall, *A Funeral Discourse, delivered in the domestic chapel of Alton Towers, after the Solemn Requiem Mass, celebrated for John, Earl of Shrewsbury* ... (London, Dolman, 1852); E. Price, 'Memoir of the late Earl of Shrewsbury', in the *Catholic Directory*, 1854, pp. 141–61; over-estimated in Gillow, *Dictionary*, V, pp. 503–5, but corrected in D. Gwynn, *Lord Shrewsbury, Pugin and the Catholic Revival* (1943), pp. 127–32.
142. He is holding the text in the portrait by Carl Blass (now at Carlton Towers, Yorkshire), posthumously issued as a print, 'John Talbot, 16th Earl of Shrewsbury, Wexford and Waterford, FSA [sic]', by Joseph Francis Aloysius Lynch: Purcell, *Phillipps*, II, pp. 321–3, 326–7, 336; Ward, *Wiseman*, I, p. 215; II, p. 254. The Society of Antiquaries has no record of his being elected Fellow.
143. For Shrewsbury's criticism of his own chaplain Dr Rock, see Shrewsbury to Pugin, March 1840, in Belcher (ed.), *Letters of Pugin*, I, p. 167. However, he left him £500 in his will.
144. *Rambler*, NS VII (1857), p. 322; *Tablet* (1858), p. 789. For George Montgomery (1827–1900) see Gillow, *Dictionary*, V, pp. 87–8.
145. *Builder* (1852), pp. 605–6; *Tablet* (1852), p. 243.
146. *Annual Register* (1852), pp. 326–7; *Illustrated London News*, (1852), 563–4; *Tablet* (1852), pp. 771, 777–8.
147. G. Crouchback to Captin Guy Crouchback, in E. Waugh, *Sword of Honour* (1978 edn), pp. 546–7.
148. *Complete Peerage*, XI, p. 727.
149. R. O'Donnell, 'The Later Pugins', in Atterbury and Wainwright, *Pugin*, pp. 259–71; R. O'Donnell, 'E. W. Pugin', in Turner (ed.), *The Grove Dictionary of Art*, XXV, pp. 716–17.
150. Below, gazetteer.
151. Below, gazetteer.
152. Below, gazetteer.
153. Below, gazetteer.

154. R. O'Donnell, 'The Kentish obituary of Edward Pugin', in *True Principles: The Voice of the Pugin Society*, Summer 2000.
155. Below, gazetteer.
156. Below, gazetteer.
157. Below, gazetteer.
158. Below, gazetteer.
159. *Tablet* (1859), p. 629; O'Donnell, 'The Later Pugins', in Atterbury and Wainwright, *Pugin*, pp. 264–6.
160. For Ullathorne's views on diocesan finances see Ullathorne, *Cabin-boy*, pp. 290–1; for his 1856 *Pastoral* see *Tablet* (1856), p. 772.
161. BAA, SC/C3/7–8, E. W. Pugin to Canon Souter, 29 April and 25 May 1874.
162. A. M. Dunn (1833–1917) and E. J. Hansom (1842–1900), architects in partnership 1871–93 in Newcastle, were responsible for the abbey church at Downside (1873–83), and Our Lady and the English Martyrs, Cambridge (1885–93).
163. M McInnally, 'St Bernard's Seminary, Olton', in Champ (ed.), *Oscott*, pp. 107–27.
164. R. O'Donnell, 'Benedictine Building in the Nineteenth Century', in Dom Geoffrey Scott, OSB (ed.), *English Benedictine Congregation History Symposium*, III (1983), pp. 38–48.
165. Although outside the two dioceses covered, Belmont is included in the gazetteer.
166. Below, gazetteer.
167. A set of drawings signed 'E. W. Pugin, Ramsgate July 1865' for 'the Chapel of Ease Sutton Coldfield for the Reverend Meredith' is in the Oscott archives.

GAZETTEER

ALTON TOWERS

The seat of the last two Catholic Earls of Shrewsbury has a very complicated building history. Charles, the 15th Earl, while retaining his main seat at Heythrop in Oxfordshire,[1] began in 1814 to transform Alton Lodge into Alton Abbey. His nephew John, who succeeded him as the 16th Earl in 1827, transformed it yet again into Alton Towers. Pugin worked at Alton from 1837 until his death; he did more here than is generally supposed, much of it furniture and decoration which no longer survives.[2] Externally, the most accessible elements of his additions are on the east and north sides, and the visual culmination is his Great Hall (1848) which, with its steep roof and spirelet, ties together the otherwise rambling north front. It is built of stone, with an enormous bay window, and steep slated roofs with much metal-work cresting and heraldry.

Internally the Hall is roofed by arched-braced king-post trusses, wind braces and boarding, all painted, with a central louvre and spire. Extraordinarily Pugin contrived this space by taking out the existing internal structure, re-roofing the whole range by adding the bay window. There is fine heraldic stained glass by Hardman & Co. here and in the south window, but the glass is partly missing; there are two fireplaces on the east wall. The buffet at the west end marking the screens' passage entrance, and the elaborate chandelier shown at the Great Exhibition, are missing.[3] The furnishings of the hall were still unfinished at the time of the 16th Earl's death, and the two fireplaces were completed only at the time of his funeral.[4] This was one of Pugin's finest evocations of the great halls of English medieval great houses. He also added at the south-east the chaplain's lodgings, the Entrance Tower to the Armoury – Talbot Gallery wing; the long screen walls to the north-east and north-west, including the barbican gate and the postern gate, a mini-fortification which he often caricatured but here made most convincing. Other Pugin work within the ruins is not accessible. E. W. Pugin also worked here for the 17th Earl.[5] Accessible by railway, the Towers attracted many tourists.[6]

1. Heythrop was burnt down in 1830 and was thereafter abandoned by the Shrewsburys: Mrs Bryan H. Stapelton, *A History of Post-Reformation Catholic Missions in Oxfordshire* (1906), pp. 142–52.
2. The complex story is now brilliantly described in M. Fisher, *Alton Towers: A Gothic Wonderland* (Stafford, 1999).
3. The chandelier is now in the House of Lords: A. Wedgwood, 'The Mediaeval Court', in P. Atterbury and C. Wainwright (eds), *Pugin*, p. 243, illus. p. 180.
4. Birmingham City Archives, Hardman Collection, Metalwork Day Book (1849–1854), f. 490, 24 December 1852, two fireplace backs, dogs etc. 'for the dining room', £100.
5. Fisher, *Alton Towers*, p. 129.
6. P. Mandler, *The Fall and Rise of the Stately Home 1837–1975* (1997), pp. 70, 86.

ALTON TOWERS, THE CHAPEL OF ST PETER

On his accession the pious 'Good Earl John' decided to replace an existing private chapel with a larger chapel in a neo-Perpendicular style (1834).[1] Although a long description of the new building appeared in the Catholic press, no architect was named; Thomas Fradgley of Uttoxeter has been suggested, as has Joseph Potter of Lichfield.[2] The chapel is built of stone with low pitched leaded roofs, and on a large scale, 90ft long by 30ft wide and 60ft high,[3] but even with its tower and turrets and pinnacles at the liturgical 'east end', it is of somewhat domestic inspiration. The three-storey interior was lit only from high up and was dramatically focused on the sanctuary. The chapel also served the local Catholic mission, and the registers date from 1820. The congregation had access to the ground floor while the Earl and his family worshipped from their own tribune or gallery at first-floor level; the Oxford don J. R. Bloxam asserted that to attend a service from here was not the same as an act of worship.[4]

Pugin made additions to the interior of the chapel, such as the 'super-altar' of seven compartments of painted panels, the tabernacle and reredos, a sort of unequal triptych with attenuated wings, similar to that which he installed at Oscott in 1838.[5] The shallow apse and the altar in the oriel window bay must have disappointed Pugin, and in 1840 he gave it further definition by flanking the arch with screenwork containing plaster figures set in a wooden niches running across to make a sort of proscenium.[6]

Pugin designed picture frames in 1849–51, made by J. Crace & Co. for massive religious paintings, adding to the devotional atmosphere.[7] Pugin repainted the cast-iron trusses and corbel angels in reds and blues, and a painted frieze and niches were added to make the interior highly polychromatic; there was also much staining and graining.[8] However, the use of such visual tricks to disguise cast-iron, and the lack of a rood screen and distinct chancel must have frustrated Pugin. The church of St Giles, Cheadle, where the Earl also worshipped, showed what his generosity and Pugin's talents could achieve. The great funeral on 14 December 1852 of the Earl, who died within two months of his architect, took place here.[9] The chapel was recorded in a watercolour of 1854 before Catholic worship ceased in 1860, and by 1862 the altar had been removed to Bromsgrove. The owners of Alton Towers are gradually restoring the shell of the chapel and the surviving interior fragments.

1. *Catholic Magazine and Review*, V (1834), pp. 662-3.
2. Fisher, *Alton Towers*, p. 95.
3. Ibid., p. 69.
4. Belcher (ed.), *Letters of Pugin*, I, p. 141, note 3.
5. *OJ*, XI (1840), 110-12.
6. Ibid., X (1840), 412; Belcher (ed.), *Letters of Pugin*, I, pp. 136-7. Michael Fisher has made a reconstruction, following a drawing of 1842 by Samuel Rayner: Fisher, *Alton Towers*, frontispiece and p. 149.
7. Wedgwood, *Pugin Family*, pp. 117, 175-6.
8. The ceiling painting was restored in 1994: Fisher, *Alton Towers*, pp. 150-1, 156.
9. R. O'Donnell, 'No "maimed rites": the funeral obsequies of the Earl of Shrewsbury, 1852', in *True Principles: The Voice of the Pugin Society*, Summer 2002, pp. 17-21.

ALTON, HOSPITAL OF ST JOHN THE BAPTIST

In Alton village the 16th Earl of Shrewsbury built the Hospital of St John the Baptist (his patronal name) and a new castle within the existing twelfth- and thirteenth-century ruins. The site on the opposite side of the Churnet gorge from Alton Towers was chosen for its picturesque relationship to the Towers. The hospital project illustrates, like Hardman's hospital in Birmingham, one type of Catholic religious response to the social problems of the age, as well as providing the physical setting for the Catholic mission in the village.[1] Literally 'hospital' meant a retreat for the old or sick, and here Pugin intended to provide a residence for priests, as well as a school. He had specific 'hospital' models, such as Brown's Hospital at Stamford and St Cross Hospital at Winchester, on which he drew for the plate 'The Antient Poorhouse' in *Contrasts* (1841).[2] However, as late as Christmas 1841 Pugin explained to Lord Shrewsbury that he was negotiating with Wiseman to house retired priests, which suggests that certain functions were still not fixed,[3] and although the church was ready and consecrated (that is, free of debt) on 13 July 1842,[4] it is clear that Pugin did not persuade Shrewsbury to establish the 'permanent foundation',[5] which would have reflected the full 'hospital' organization and provided for the future of the buildings.

Alton Hospital was described and illustrated in Pugin's *Present State* (1843).[6] The design of 1839–40 is, unusually for Pugin, in a neo-Perpendicular style, which he was shortly to disown, and he did not complete this scheme. It has three ranges open to the west and to Alton Castle. On the north side is the church, and on the south the school or Guildhall. The red sandstone was from the Counslow quarry on the Alton estate; the roof tiles and the richly detailed metalwork and leadwork are all expensive materials. The church has an enclosing walled churchyard to the east and to the south a stone crucifix on a plinth. The three-storey tower adjacent to the church contains a diminutive house for the resident chaplain with a spiral staircase to the chaplain's rooms above, illustrating Pugin's highly coloured conception of how the clergy should live. Ground-floor sacristies and central entrance corridor connect with an L-plan cloister, which continues on an irregular plan to the main residential range on the east. This has a central gabled entrance, with ground-floor chambers or shared rooms, and cells above for 'decayed priests'. The range continues to the south, evidently intended for some community use, but individual elements are increasingly difficult to reconstruct. Was the three-arched opening on the outer south face (now opening into the schoolyard) intended as an entrance to a refectory (Pugin's engraving shows a hall and kitchen) but in a different position? The actual three-storey range was largely complete by 1849, as was the Guidhall with a spired stair-tower, which now serves as the charmingly old-fashioned Catholic primary school. The buildings were incomplete on Pugin's death, when they were described as 'a hospital for decayed priests ... designed by the late Mr Pugin [the] unfinished portions now progressing under the direction of Mr Edward Pugin'.[7]

The church has a nave, which on weekdays was used as a school or 'school-chapel'; Pugin described how the 'seats in the school ... are made with desks which *fall down* and

A. W. N. Pugin, 'The Present Revival of Christian Architecture', frontispiece to *The Apology for the Revival of Christian Architecture* (1843). Thirty-five of his church commissions – more than fifty since 1838 – are shown; Alton Hospital is at the top left and St Giles, Cheadle bottom right; the lodge at Oscott is centre foreground.

A. W. N. Pugin, *The Glossary of Ecclesiastical Ornament* (1844), frontispiece. Pugin proposed to involve all the arts in the Catholic Revival. However, as a handbook to his teachings, the *Glossary* was impractical.

Pugin's revolution centred on the liturgy: an anonymous sketch, St Cuthbert's College Ushaw, contrasts the so-called 'Gothic' mass vestments (centre), which Pugin re-introduced, with those from Rome (left) or France (right; a 'Gallican priest') found in the Regency Catholicism he so ruthlessly guyed in his early journalism.

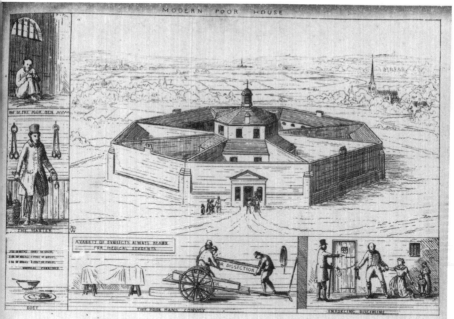

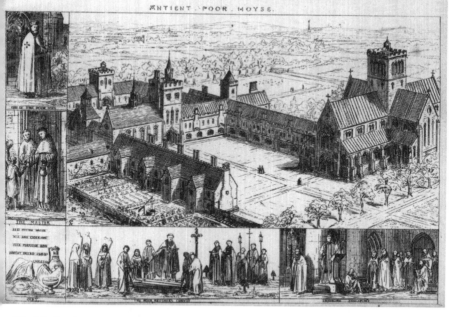

. W. N. Pugin, 'Contrasted residences for the Poor': *Contrasts* (1841). The work-
ouses set up under the 1834 Poor Law are contrasted with the lavish buildings of a
'hospital' based on that of St Cross, Winchester.

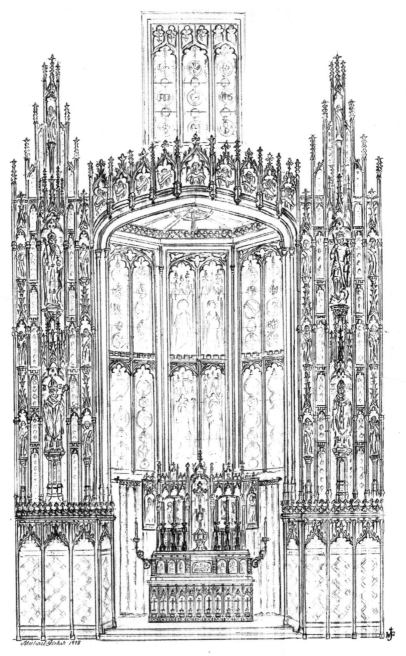

ALTON TOWERS CHAPEL
REREDOS AND SCREEN BY A. WELBY PUGIN c 1840

Alton Towers Chapel: interior reconstruction drawing by the Revd M. Fisher, 1998

The funeral of the Earl of Shrewsbury in the Chapel of St Peter, Alton Towers, 14 December 1852.

Alton Hospital of St John the Baptist: the chapel, from *Present State*.

Alton Hospital of St John the Baptist: A. W. N. Pugin's bird's-eye view from *Prese*
State (1843); the function of the central ranges was still undecided when this drawi
was made.

Alton Castle from the south (1843–56); the function of the castle is still not clear.

Left: Banbury, St John the
Baptist: *c.* 1910,
showing fittings
attributed to Pugin.

Below: The interior.

Right: Belmont: the Abbey Church and monastic buildings.

Below: The Abbey Church: nave and crossing.

Belmont Abbey Hereford.
The Abbey Church from the West Door.

Left: Belmont Abbey, the monastic choir and sanctuary, largely destroyed or altered after 1953.

Below: The high altar and reredos carved by R. L. Boulton (1865–66). The altar was destroyed in the 1970s.

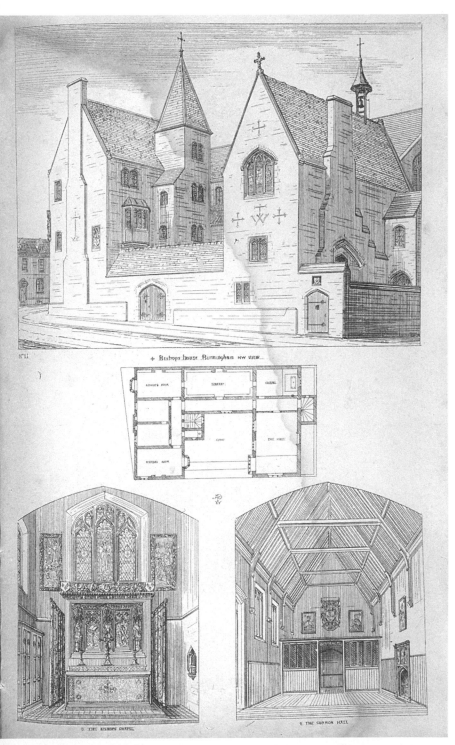

Birmingham, the Bishop's House (demolished): Pugin's drawing from *Present State*.

Birmingham, St Chad's Cathedral: Pugin's rood screen (1840–1), re-arranged in thi
form in 1854, was demolished and disposed of in 1967 despite assurances that it woul
be retained.

The sanctuary, 1904.

The exterior, isolated in the 1960s road layout, c. 1978.

St Mary's College, Oscott: Pugin's etching of the interior, drawn in 1837, anticipated the installation of antique and of neo-Gothic furnishings.

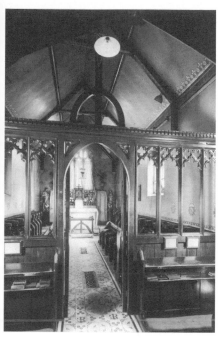

Handsworth, Convent of Mercy: the chapel (sanctuary destroyed 1941).

Nechells, St Joseph: the chancel.

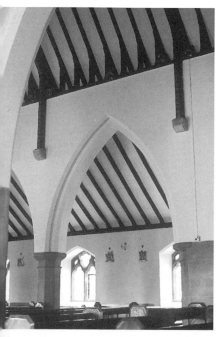

Brewood, St Mary: the nave arcade and south aisle.

Brewood, St Mary: the font, *c.* 1844.

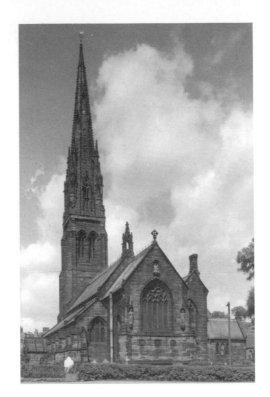

Cheadle, St Giles: the east end.

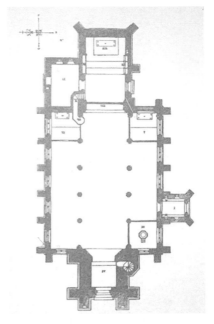

Cheadle, St Giles: plan.

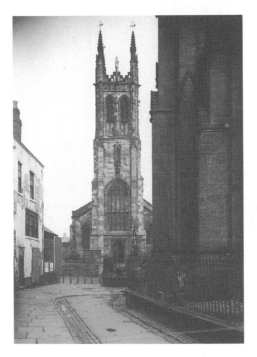

Derby, St Mary: the church from Bridge Gate, *c*. 1964.

The interior as furnished with metal screen and pulpit by E. W. Pugin and J. H. Powell in 1855: photo before 1930.

Garendon: the stairs hall as reformed by E. W. Pugin after 1864; the bust on the left is of Ambrose Phillipps de Lisle.

Grace Dieu Manor from the south. Pugin's family wing is to the right.

Grace Dieu Manor, the interior of the chapel *c.* 1878. Pugin refurnished the chapel in 1840, the chancel was truncated *c.* 1900; all the furnishings were destroyed or disposed of 1962–5 by Grace Dieu Manor School.

Grace Dieu Manor School: the chapel *c.* 1947.

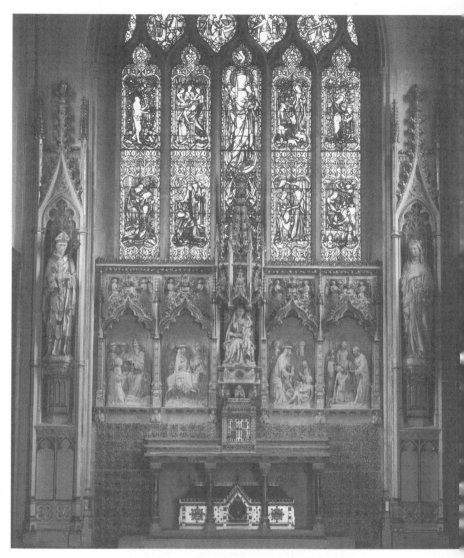

Henley, Sacred Heart: the east end ensemble (*c.* 1850–56) of the altar and reredos, by the Pugins, with the J. H. Powell window (1862) were re-assembled by A. S. G. Butler, architect (1936). Proposals to dismantle the altar were made in 2000 and 2002.

Mount St Bernard Abbey, Leicestershire: Pugin's drawings in *Present State* (1843).

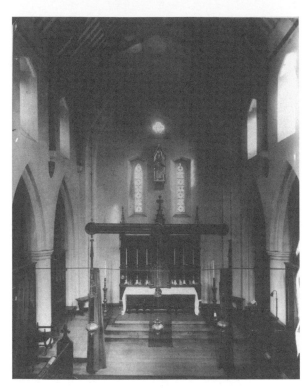

Left: Mount St Bernard Abbey, Leicestershire: the abbey church interior *c*. 1878. None of the fittings are by Pugin.

Below: Mount St Bernard Abbey: the guest wing *c*. 1880.

Nottingham, St Barnabas' Cathedral: sanctuary.

The south transept with the chancel south aisle (left) and the Blessed Sacrament chapel (right). Photograph after 1932; largely altered after 1965.

A. W. N. Pugin's scheme as published in *Present State* (1843).

Ratcliffe College, Leicester: Pugin's scheme of *c.* 1843.

The east front (1842–47) *c.* 1962. The left-hand gable and return is by C. F. Hansom.

Ratcliffe College, Leicester *c*. 1947. E. W. Pugin's chapel in foreground.

Right: The chapel *c*. 1945.
The interior was
destroyed in 1962.

Solihull, St Augustine: the exterior before 1977.

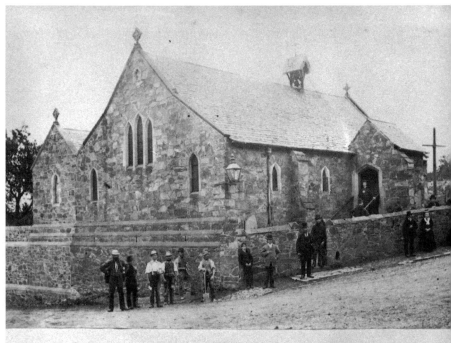

St.Winefred's Church, Shepshed. *Erected 1842.*

Shepshed, former church of St Winefred. The east end *c.* 1878. The photograph record
the addition on the left.

Spetchley, Worcestershire: The School (1841), showing the two-storey schoolmaster's house and schoolrooms, chapel to right.

Stafford: Burton Manor, from the south-west. The house (1855–6) was E. W. Pugin's first domestic commission.

Stanbrook Abbey, Worcestershire: E. W. Pugin's drawing for an unexecuted church.

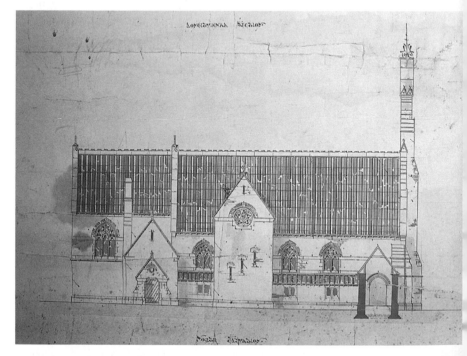

E. W. Pugin's drawing of the church as executed.

Stanbrook Abbey: the church interior before 1935.

Stone, Staffordshire, Chapel of St Anne: exterior *c*. 1978.

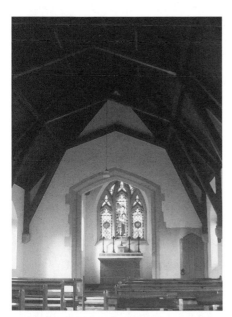

Chapel of St Anne: interior, *c*. 1978.

Stone, Oulton St Mary's Abbey:
interior, *c*. 1930.

Wymeswold, Church of St Mary (Anglican): the north porch added by Pugin.

Uttoxeter, Church of St Mary: Pugin's sanctuary as published in 1838.

Henley, Sacred Heart: Pugin drawings *c.* 1850 for the figures of St Charles Borromeo and St Elizabeth of Hungary. Myers' 'men' were expected to work direc from such sketches; the figures as executed are more elaborate.

St Mary's College, Oscott: Pugin's drawing (1837) shows the roof plan, sections an details of bosses he installed in the apse which had been designed by Messrs Robert the architects.

become capital church seats for sundays & holidays'.[8] Pugin
had to defend the cost of the stained glass to Lord Shrewsbury: 'When your lordship sees the glorious effect of the
Glass in the school room you will not blame me. It is not
for the urchins but for the elite who will flock to see the
building ... a perfect specimen of the style.'[9] The floors
were laid in quarry tiles 'excepting where the benches are
... & I thought it would be too cold for the children'.[10]
There is a deep chancel or choir, and a sanctuary with a side
chapel off to the north. The pulpit, bracketed out from the
juntion of nave and chancel, is a favourite Pugin device. The
font is also by Pugin. The wooden rood screen, the loss of
which Archbishop Grimshaw refused to agree to as late as
1963, was removed *c*.1967 at the insistence of Archbishop
Dwyer, much to the distress of the Mercy Sisters who had
taken over the buildings; it is currently stored at the Birmingham City Art Gallery and Museum.[11] The floriated crucifix now hangs in the arch, but the associated figures of the
Blessed Virgin and St John are currently detached. The
screen was a particular loss since the quality of the woodwork is the highest of any Pugin church, as the elaborately
carved poppy head and pierced-backed oak choir benches
(some currently in the nave) show. Happily there is a scheme
to return the rood screen. The alabaster high altar and the
reredos (now detached) are both part-painted and gilt. The
carving is of high quality, particularly the central bas-relief
of the altar front; Pugin supplied an antique crucifix for the
altar and made candlesticks to match.[12] The east window
c.1840, by William Willement, is of three lights depicting
Shrewsbury's patron saints, with flanking statues of saints in
niches. The elaborate collar-truss braces of the nave roof are
further elaborated in the sanctuary, but the colouring
described in *Present State*[13] no longer survives. There are
brasses by Hardman & Co. to the 16th and 17th Earls, on
either side of high altar,[14] but the materials and levels of the
sanctuary floor were altered *c*.1967. Other Hardman brasses
to members of the Talbot family of Co. Wexford and to the
15th Earl are to be found in the cloister.

Next to the sanctuary is a chantry-like chapel. It has a lean-to-arch vaulted roof and houses what looks like a founder's tomb, a favourite Pugin furnishing, under a four-centred arch niche with much heraldry. The function of an iron cupboard door on its inner face is unclear but might relate to use as an Easter Sepulchre. The Blessed Sacrament iconography of the diminutive alabaster altar shows its intended use for daily reservation. There is a squint to the main sanctuary. This is a perfect example of Pugin's exquisite handling of small-scale design: as he said to Lord Shrewsbury, 'the small chapel of the sepulchre looks 400 hundred years old'.[15]

Pugin also adapted a seventeenth-century cottage to function as a schoolmaster's house, with walls and gate-piers, c.1841, and the addition of a porch, two elaborate external chimney-breasts, a single-storey kitchen or office range, a garden wall and two privies.[16] It is an interesting example of his vernacular style. Further social and religious provision was made as the building campaign wound on into the careers of Bertram, the 17th Earl, and of Edwin Pugin, turning Alton village into a perfect little Catholic world. As Pugin wrote to Lord Shrewsbury: 'Nobody now *dies* a protestant at Alton if they do not all live Catholics.'[16] The local Anglican vicar and the neighbouring curate issued hostile pamphlets accusing the Catholics of prose-lytism, to which Lord Shrewsbury replied with *An Address to the Inhabitants of Alton* (1842);[17] no doubt the (Anglican) 'Alton National School' was built in riposte in 1845.

1. S. J. Gosling, *A Short Account . . . of St John the Baptist Alton* (Coventry, c.1951); D. Higham and P. Carson, *Pugin's Churches of the Second Spring: An Historical Guide to the Catholic Churches of Cheadle, Alton and Cotton* (Uttoxeter, 1997), pp. 46–52.
2. Plate 'the Antient Poorhouse' in 'Contrasted Residences of the Poor'.
3. Belcher (ed.), *Letters of Pugin*, I, pp. 306–8.
4. Ibid., p. 361, note 7.
5. Ibid., pp. 297–9.
6. Plate no. V, and pp. 92–5. See also *Tablet* (1848), p. 453.
7. *Tablet* (1852), p. 803.

8. Belcher (ed.), *Letters of Pugin*, I, p. 270.
9. Ibid., p. 276.
10. Ibid., p. 321.
11. BAA, P69/8/19–24, correspondence between Mgr Fay and Archbishop Grimshaw.
12. *Present State*, p. 94; Belcher (ed.), *Letters of Pugin*, I, p. 227.
13. *Present State*, p. 93.
14. Birmingham City Archives, Hardman Collection, Metalwork Day Book, (1854–57) f. 246.
15. Belcher (ed.), *Letters of Pugin*, I, p. 227.
16. Ibid., p. 306.
17. BAA, P69/8/2, *An Address by Lord Shrewsbury*, 4 July 1842, in reply to the Revd John Pike, *An Address to the Inhabitants of Alton*.

ALTON CASTLE

On the adjacent crag to the Hospital stands Alton Castle. The east tower wall and south curtain wall are late twelfth-century, and the gatehouse and western tower walls are thirteenth-century. Pugin began building at the Castle in 1842,[1] but it was left incomplete. The function of the new castle is disputed; the plan and scale imply retreat and privacy rather than display and hospitality for the 16th Earl and his entourage. Perhaps it was to be a dower house, or for unmarried members of the Earl's immediate family, or for Bertram, his second cousin and heir. Although there was popular suspicion that it was to be yet another Catholic monastery, Pugin hotly denounced the idea that it was to be 'a castle for priests', as his retort to Lord Shrewsbury shows: 'This Castle at Alton has made me sick at heart after writing a book against mock Castles . . . you call on me to violate every principle & build a Castle <u>for priests!!!!</u>'[2] Late into the building campaign Shrewsbury suggested further sources for the design, to which Pugin replied with characteristic vigour: 'Nothing can be more dangerous than looking at prints of buildings and trying to imitate bits of them. These architectural books are as bad as the scriptures in the hands of Protestants.'[3] Built in the fine local Counslow stone, the castle comprises a two-storey left-hand or stateroom range with stair-tower and belfry, and a four-storey right-hand wing with two stair-towers; where the two ranges join up is the projecting chapel. Shrewsbury was interested in the historic layout and archaeology of the site, so the chapel was built above an existing medieval crypt and the two ranges at right angles are like lodging ranges in a medieval castle. The angle towers, and the high gable, ridgeline and apse of the chapel form a highly romantic skyline. Much of the interior is finished in dressed stone-ashlar, such as the corridors, the stairs, the central lobby, which forms an ante-chapel, and the dramatic three-storey stone-vaulted chapel beyond. There is a sacristy, and a room above with a squint view into the chapel, possibly serving as a sort of watching chamber. The stained glass is post-1945 with iconography of the Mercy Sisters who arrived here in 1855 and ran a preparatory school from the 1890s, with some amusing scenes of the history of the site, including Pugin on scaffolding. The Castle became the Archdiocesan Youth Centre in 1996 and regrettably the chapel was stripped of its furnishings and is not currently used for Mass.

In the east range there are three chambers with stone fire-places on the ground floor and a pair of chambers on the floor above; these were decorated not by Pugin but by Alton estate craftsmen after 1856. At the south end is the fine oriel window overlooking the hospital. The north range is much more utilitarian, with rooms off corridors on three floors. On the ground floor is a triple-arched kitchen fireplace; further service rooms were contained in natural vaults in the rock below. Overall the Castle remains an enigma, another example of the *folie-de-batir* of the 16th Earl.[4]

1. Belcher (ed.), *Letters of Pugin*, I, pp. 325–6.
2. Pugin to Shrewsbury 30 July 1847, quoted in Wedgwood, *Pugin Family*, p. 111.
3. Pugin to Shrewsbury, ?25 April 1843, ibid., p. 20.
4. M. Girouard, 'Alton Castle', in *Country Life*, 238 (1960), p. 1226; Girouard, *The Victorian Country House* (1979 edn), pp. 47–8, 394.

BANBURY, ST JOHN THE BAPTIST

This ambitious stone-built Gothic church is by Hinckman & Derrick of Oxford, architects (1833–8).[1] It appears to be the result of three campaigns by its priests, Pierre Hersent, a French émigré priest, who moved the mission here from nearby Warkworth (just over the Northamptonshire boundary) in 1828, dying in 1833 (he is commemorated in a Puginesque brass showing him in medieval Mass vestments); Joseph Fox who 'added the tower and walls to the church' (1833–5), and Dr William Tandy, 'who completed . . . this church in 1838'.[2] Although the chancel and its furnishings were described in the Catholic press[3] without identifying Pugin, it is first mentioned in his diary in 1838.[4] The high altar candlesticks, similar to those he gave to Oscott at this date, are probably from a metalwork order first supplied in 1838. The windows and their tracery, the grisaille glass and stained glass with a kneeling donor,[5] and orders for an altar, pulpit and other furniture in 1841 can all safely be attributed to Pugin.[6] Historic photographs showing a rood beam and figures also suggest Pugin's hand. The presbytery adjacent (but not the schools) is also highly Puginesque.[7]

1. Mrs Bryan H. Stapelton, *A History of Post Reformation Catholic Missions in Oxfordshire* (1906), pp. 41–5.
2. Inscription on Tandy's monument.
3. *Catholic Magazine*, NS II (1838), p. 501; *OJ*, VII (1838), 18; A. G. Wall, *Guide to St John's* (Banbury, 1936).
4. Pugin's Diary 28 September 1838, in Wedgwood, *Pugin Family*, pp. 40, 81. It is also mentioned in 1840 and 1841.
5. Belcher (ed.), *Letters of Pugin*, I, pp. 267–8.
6. Ibid., p. 267; Pugin's Diary 1841, Wedgwood, *Pugin Family*, p. 51.
7. Stanton, *Pugin*, p. 198, gives the chancel to Pugin.

BELMONT, THE ABBEY CHURCH OF ST MICHAEL AND ALL ANGELS, AND MONASTERY

The abbey church at Belmont is one of E. W. Pugin's best but least known churches. It may have had a particular significance for him, and he seems to have treated it as one of his most personal commissions. Begun in 1854, with nave and aisles, crossing and a lower sanctuary, the church is the product of several building campaigns, starting in the west and progressing successively eastwards.[1] The magnificent site was presented by the patron, Francis Richard Wegg-Prosser of Belmont House, a recent Catholic convert. Wegg-Prosser had vowed to build a Benedictine monastery here and he probably paid for the earlier stages of building (the finance for the later stages came from the Benedictines themselves).[2] While still an Anglican, he had commissioned E. W. Pugin's earliest building on the site, a school-chapel of 1853 that was to mark the start of the Catholic presence on the estate.[3] The chapel served as a school during the week and as a church on Sunday. Hardman supplied metalwork for this chapel, such as altar fittings and a chalice, to E. W. Pugin's order.[4]

In 1855 E. W. Pugin exhibited his scheme for the abbey church at the Royal Academy.[5] Further building work took place in 1857 and 1860, and again in 1865, when the original sanctuary was rebuilt as an aisled choir and the transepts were added.[6] Then in 1869 the choir roof was raised, the aisles were extended with east chapels, and two further sanctuary bays were added. Drawings show that E. W. Pugin first considered a single-bay extension in 1867.[7] At each stage in the development of the building the original east window and much of the stonework of the east gable were taken down and re-erected further east, giving the church something of the organic feel of a many-phased medieval church. The position and function of certain parts of the church changed with bewildering frequency; thus the St Benedict chapel of 1862 is now reached through the 1869 extension. A north porch replaced the original south porch, and the latter is now occupied as a war memorial chapel. The south door off the transept now communicates through an inner porch and corridor with the monastery and its sacristies. The church was completed in 1881–2 by Peter Paul Pugin, who added the belfry and the battlemented stage of the tower.[8] But a bird's-eye 'eastwards' perspective (one of a pair preserved in the monastery) signed Pugin, Ashlin & Pugin and dated 1878, shows that a much more ambitious completion scheme had been contemplated, with two western towers, a central crossing tower and many more monastery buildings.[9]

The church is built of beautiful local reddish-grey sandstone with lighter yellow sandstone dressings under prominent slated roofs. Internally it is lined with ravishing ashlar stone embellished with high quality carving. So close is the west part of the church to his father's style that E. W. Pugin might have been working from reused drawings or casts of medieval details. The nave arcades, the tracery details and the trussed roof are a definite homage to A. W. Pugin's St Augustine's at Ramsgate, where his father told him: 'I am giving you the best architectural training I can; watch the church, there shall not be a single "true principle" broken.'[10]

Elsewhere we see the young architect beginning to branch out in a more personal direction. This can be seen in the large tracery windows in the three main gables – particularly the west window with its cross shape set within a circle – and in the side windows of the sanctuary under their stone cross-gables. There are three types of piers and arches: the traditional neo-fourteenth-century type in the nave and crossing; the squatter piers of the choir with their naturalistic capitals and stilted arches 'dying' into the imposts; and the slim attenuated piers with abstract bases, scalloped capitals and simplified arches of the sanctuary. (The carved angels playing musical instruments on the choir capitals were probably carved by the Cheltenham sculptor R. L. Boulton.) The roof forms also develop from the expensively detailed wooden trusss and wind braces of the nave, through the stone vault of the crossing – both close to Ramsgate types – to the heavily trussed, panelled and part gabled form of the choir, and the heavy wooden cornice, arched trusses and panels with bosses of the sanctuary.

E. W. Pugin gave considerable thought to lighting the east end, as he moved away from the cell-like plan and low light levels of his father's models, so that the finally achieved sanctuary of 1869 is dramatically end-lit and side-lit. Pairs of large, deep windows are set in the bays formed by reducing the thickness of the side walls and inserting a single polychrome stone column (now painted one colour); the walls and arches are lined in alabaster. This was specifically intended to highlight the climax of the church, the high altar. The altar itself was an example of the 'open' type that E. W. Pugin developed at Danesfield *c.*1853–6[11] and then at Stanbrook in 1868.[12] The working part, the mensa, was an openwork design of columns supporting the simple slab, with a reliquary chest beneath (this survives in storage in the monastery). Set to the rear of the altar slab was a gradine, and within it a square-profiled tabernacle. Unlike E. W. Pugin's 'benediction altars', it did not have an elaborate 'throne' or spire, but instead a sort of removable superstructure – a crown-like termination, worked in metal, and now displayed on the Lady altar. Carved by R. L. Boulton, the altar was made up in two parts, the first in 1865 and the reredos in 1866. The latter is a magnificent example of Boulton's skill, with choirs of demi-figure angels holding musical instruments in swooning states of adoration centred over the position of the tabernacle, above which two angels hold a projecting stone crown.[13] 'Rationalized' in the 1950s, the high altar was destroyed in the 1970s, when the layout of the church was turned through 180 degrees, from east to west. Only the reredos survives, hanging incongruously above some crudely designed marble panels from the John Hardman Studio, installed in 1978–9 when the original orientation was reinstated by the Hereford architects McClennan, Johnson, Blight. The freestanding altar under the tower, stone floor and nave benches also date from this period, and now cry out for replacement.[14]

The church was gradually furnished with lavish altars, screens, statues, and tombs, in stone, alabaster, marble, brass, iron, wood and encaustic tile, but Benedictine views on liturgical simplicity together with the popular anti-Victorianism of the post-war years led to the stripping out of much of this furniture as early as 1953. Among the casualities was the screen inserted by Pugin & Pugin in 1882 to make a chantry chapel in the north transept for Thomas Joseph Brown, OSB, Vicar Apostolic of Wales (1840–50), then first Bishop of Newport and Menevia (1850–80) in the restored Hierarchy, whose ornate tomb stands below the main window. At the same time an altar and reredos to St David against the east wall of the transept was destroyed to make room for the neo-Renaissance tomb of Brown's successor, John Cuthbert Hedley, OSB (bishop 1881–1915), which had originally been sited in the choir between the monks' stalls, a striking neo-medieval conceit. There are important chapels and partly surviving altars to St Joseph (north choir aisle), Our Lady, (south choir aisle) and St Benedict, the latter reached through a stone screen off the south choir aisle.

Much expensive Hardman stained glass was installed from the 1850s onwards: the east window of St Michael and the Angel Host by J. H. Powell (dated 1860) moved eastwards with each phase of rebuilding to reach its current location in 1869; the west window, also by Powell, of St Thomas Cantiloupe and other saints of Hereford interest (c.1880 or later). Other fittings of note are the statues of Our Lady and of the Sacred Heart (papier mâché, painted and gilt, by Mayer & Co. of Munich, c.1870); the Hardman & Co. brass lectern of c.1873; the stalls, by Bryant & Cotes of Cheltenham, 1879, incorporating parts of earlier stalls (the fine fronts designed by Lady Butler); the organ case, 1889; a relic of the True Cross (in a Belgian setting?) c.1880; and the Abbot's throne, 1959 (a copy of the Bishop's throne transferred to Cardiff Cathedral). Of the surviving E. W. Pugin's drawings in the archive, many are for metalwork, much of which was 'command' rather than catalogue work for this church.[15]

E. W. Pugin also built the two-storey, high-pitched roofed, E-plan monastery range (1857–9), in what he described as the 'Modern Gothic' style in 1859.[16] By this he meant a somewhat rationalist Gothic Revival manner, with big sash windows rather than poky casements, broad corridors and good ventilation, attenuated proportions and steep roofs. The monastery then is not a picturesque evocation of the Middle Ages such as A. W. Pugin preferred, but something very mid-Victorian. Even more 'Modern Gothic' is the large, villa-like lodging for Bishop Brown of 1865, with additions in 1867.[17] There is a fine refectory. Peter Paul Pugin added an infirmary range in 1880, and designed a home farm, recently adapted for housing. The undated 'westward' bird's-eye drawing by Pugin & Pugin shows even more elaborate monastery wings.

All this ambitious building was called for since Belmont was set up in 1859 to be the central novitiate for the English Congregation of the Benedictine Order. The buildings and the church, where the young monks were to develop their *esprit-de-l'âme*, were meant to be lavish, much more so than the then modest chapels which served houses such as Downside or Ampleforth, to which they returned after the formative years at Belmont.[18] This function lasted until 1917, and in 1920 Belmont became an independent abbey. From 1859 until 1916 it was the pro-Cathedral of Newport and Menevia.[19] The monastery ran a school until recently, but now performs other pastoral work.

1. *Builder* (1854), p. 193.
2. *Catholic Directory* (1854).
3. B. W. Kelly, *English Catholic Missions* (1908), pp. 73–4, says £17,000 was spent. E. W. Pugin also rebuilt Belmont House for Wegg-Prosser *c.*1870.
4. Birmingham City Archives, Hardman Collection, Metalwork Day Book (1849–54), 29 January 1853, altar fittings £51; 22 July 1853 chalice, missal etc. £23.
5. *Builder* (1855), pp. 229, 293, 299.
6. Ibid. (1857), p. 408; (1860), p. 662.
7. Belmont Abbey, uncatalogued collection of architectural drawings.
8. *The Architect* (1882), p. 133.
9. Belmont Abbey drawings.
10. A. Wedgwood (ed.), 'J. H. Powell, *"Pugin in his home"* *c.*1884', in *Architectural History* (Journal of the Society of Architectural Historians, GB), 31 (1998), pp. 170–205, quote p. 194.
11. Below, gazetteer, under Henley.

12. Below, gazetteer.
13. *Tablet* (1866), pp. 502, 506.
14. Drawings by McClennan, Johnson, Blight, dated 1978, are in the monastery library.
15. *Belmont Abbey* (1993); R. O'Donnell, 'Notes for the Pugin Society tour 12–16 July 2000'.
16. *Builder* (1857), p. 408; (1860), p. 662.
17. Many drawings by E. W. Pugin for Bishop Brown survive in the monastery.
18. R. O'Donnell, 'Benedictine Building in the Nineteenth Century', in Dom Geoffrey Scott, OSB (ed.), *English Benedictine Congregation History Symposium*, III (1983), pp. 38–48.
19. Dom Basil Hemphill, OSB, *The History of Belmont Abbey* (1959).

BILSTON, HOLY TRINITY

In 1846 Pugin added the chancel, with its three-light stained glass window by William Wails of Newcastle-upon-Tyne,[1] to the existing church (1832–4). Pugin's screen was demolished in 1948.[2]

1. *Tablet* (1846), p. 537. Sketches from Pugin's scheme are in the Myers Family Album (private collection).
2. Anon., *The History of Holy Trinity Church Bilston* (1969), pp. 4–5, 11.

BIRMINGHAM, ST CHAD'S CATHEDRAL

Pugin's cathedral (1839–41) was built on a sloping site above the canal in the crowded gun-makers' quarter; the Bishop's House was opposite.[1] The setting was destroyed in the 1960s by the inner ring road. The church was based on German Baltic brick architecture of the Late Gothic period which Pugin, explaining his first scheme, described as 'a foreign style of pointed architecture because it is both cheap and effective and Likewise because it is totally different from any

protestant errection. Any person would be aware this was a
Catholic church at first sight . . .'[2] To show his rejection of
Georgian building habits, Pugin built in English-bond brick,
'not Flemish-bond like the hated Georgians'.[3] The church has
a sublimely successful east-end massing of slate roofs and
gables rising over a massive crypt. The window tracery varies
from Geometric to English Decorated, and overall the balance
of window to wall is just right. The obviously cathedralesque,
formal symmetry of the west front, with its doors, west
window and pair of towers and spires, is less inventive.
Various details such as the west front sculpture and the door
hinges are charming, if not as convincing as Pugin was later
to be. At this early stage of his career Pugin drew up a full
set of contract drawings for his builder George Myers and for
Bishop Walsh, although the functions shown on the drawings
were modified in execution.[4] A school was originally
proposed for the crypt which became exclusively a place of
burial[5] – Pugin hailed it as 'the first fully Catholic place of
sepulture to be revived'[6] – with elaborately furnished and
painted chantry chapels for the cathedral's major financial
supporters. The most important of these chapels is the
Hardman chantry dedicated to St John the Evangelist, which
is under the Lady Chapel. The stencilling on the walls probably dates from 1877; the altar and screen survive. Pugin's
second wife, Louisa (d.1844), is buried here. St Peter's, the
main chapel under the apse, is neo-Norman in style; in an
attempt to suggest an earlier historical pedigree to the fourteenth-century style church above; the painted decoration of
the entrance arch survives from Pugin's time.[7]

On entering the upper church from the west end one immediately feels the inspiration of the German 'hall churches'
(*hallen kirchen*), with the nave and aisles divided by the
dizzily attenuated columns supporting the continuous, single-
pitch roof. The clarity of the space is in strong contrast to the
additive plan inspired by English parish churches, which
Pugin quickly came to prefer. The principal member of the
nave roof is a queen-post truss, supported on wall posts rising
from the main piers; Pugin delighted in thus exposing the full

drama of the height and structure of his roofs as a reaction to the Georgian habit of plastering ceilings. He also liked to pare the members down to a minimum, and C. L. Eastlake's accusation that 'he starved his roof-tree to gild his altar'[8] is to misunderstand his daring. The crossing, transept and sanctuary roofs are all different so that, understood in conjunction with the carefully placed furnishings, the subdivision of the interior, which Pugin thought so essential, was achieved. It was this attenuated, elongated Continental Gothic style which appealed to twentieth-century architectural critics, antagonistic though they still were to the archaeological and moral seriousness of the Pugin period. Victorian critics, such as Eastlake[9] and Canon Greaney,[10] emphasized the furnishings. For Pugin the furniture, with its architectural and liturgical implications, was perhaps more important even than the fabric itself, and he was quite emphatic that 'in my great church in Birmingham all the ornament is within'.[11] The most important fitting was the elaborate barrier between the church and the sanctuary made by the great rood screen, Pugin's *chef d'oeuvre*, consisting of a solid dado, a traceried screen and loft, the gift of John Hardman senior.[12] Its obvious interference with sight-lines between the altar and congregation led to the first threat to its future by Bishop Wiseman in 1841; Pugin felt 'stabbed to the heart'[13] and threatened not only his resignation but the withdrawal of the Hardmans' support from the building. Wiseman was side-tracked, and the screen survived, although moved forward in 1854 to accommodate the choir founded by Hardman junior; the choir still flourishes.[14] The pulpit, repositioned on the north side in 1967, is medieval; bought through the antique trade, but traceable to the abbey church of St Gertrude in Louvain, it was presented by Lord Shrewsbury in 1841.[15] He also gave the fifteenth-century brass lectern, later moved to Oscott, and now in the Cloisters Museum in New York.[16] The canons' stalls were said to be from Sta Maria in Capitol, Cologne, as were parts of the bishop's throne and tester; Pugin added a spire 30 feet high (removed in 1967), typical of his mixing of antique fragments and new work.[17]

For Pugin rood screens were the 'grand division between priest and people',[18] a focus rather than a barrier within the church, separating not only the altar with its tabernacle but here in addition the relics of St Chad from the rest of the church. The relics, preserved by a prebendary of Lichfield at the Reformation, remained in Catholic hands, and although lost in the early nineteenth century were found by accident in 1839.[19] Pugin housed them in a gilt wood reliquary but this seems to have been replaced by a larger chest with crowning spirework and a half figure of the saint, a twentieth-century elaboration on Pugin themes.[20] He placed it on top of the reredos above the high altar, under a magnificent wooden painted and gilt baldachin, with red relief and a blue star-studded ceiling, based on the tomb of Robert the Wise in St Chiara in Naples.[21] The high altar and retable are stone, carved, painted and gilt, under the baldachin, hung with red cloth of gold textiles, between four riddle posts with their kneeling angels. On the altar, the 'big six' silver-plated candlesticks were given in 1854;[22] the cross has an earlier crucifix and is by Pugin.[23] The tabernacle, recently recased to its 1878 dimensions, with the Agony in the Garden enamels to the doors, is an example of the development of the Pugin style by J. H. Powell.[24] The whole ensemble is one of the most important mid-nineteenth-century recreations of medieval furnishings, comparable to the throne ensemble in the House of Lords.

The 1967–8 re-ordering, by Weightmann & Bullen, disposed of the screen and some other furnishings and the built-up floor levels of Pugin's sanctuary so that a forward altar on a high platform could extend out into the crossing.[25] Disastrously, Pugin's tiled floors were replaced by an inappropriate marble flooring. A coloured encaustic tiled floor on Puginesque lines by Image Ceramics has since been installed, and the rood cross and crucifixus figure, ejected along with the screen in 1967, has been re-hung (but without its attendant figures of the Virgin and St John). The screen itself has since been re-used in an Anglican church – Holy Trinity, Reading; other Pugin fittings have been sold and dispersed.[26]

Pugin's multicoloured flooring was matched by painted and stained woodwork, stencilled walls and ceilings, and magnificent stained glass. William Warrington made the three apse windows in 1840, to Pugin's design, reproducing exactly the awkward style of the thirteenth-century models at Tewkesbury Abbey and paid for by Lord Shrewsbury.[27] The Lady Chapel was designed originally in a Perpendicular style but was actually furnished in a fourteenth-century Decorated style as Pugin distanced himself from the 'late' styles with which he began. Its oak screens and altar survive. Pugin, who preferred small tabernacles and separate Blessed Sacrament chapels, provided a small 'tower' tabernacle here.[28] Pugin gave the fifteenth-century German statue of the Blessed Virgin, the model for that at Oscott.[29] The ledger brass outside to John Bernard Hardman, records family members buried in the chantry chapel below. The tomb of Bishop Walsh, shown at the Great Exhibition in 1851,[30] is one of the best examples of the extremely high quality of architectural sculpture produced by Myers from Pugin's drawings.[31] Its metal railings have recently been reinstated.

The baptistery has three two-light windows of the life of St Patrick (1843), the life of St Thomas Becket (given by Bishop Walsh) and the life of St James, with appropriate medieval lay and clerical dress; its dense colouring is obviously by William Wailes of Newcastle.[32] The font from Myers's workshop now stands outside in the aisle; its cover is missing.

From 1848 St Chad's, starting with two windows on the sanctuary south side (since replaced), was filled with stained glass by Hardman & Co. Two of the most interesting windows are on the north side. The 'glass-makers' window of 1853 in the sanctuary, given by 'the workmen, painters etc. in the works . . . at a cost of £27 15s 0d', shows four craftsmen and their trades; it was shown at the Dublin Exhibition of 1853.[33] In the north transept is the Immaculate Conception window of 1867, designed by John Hardman Powell; it shows his development after succeeding Pugin in 1852 as chief stained glass designer for Hardman & Co.[34] It is a memorial to John Hardman junior who founded, directed and endowed with

£1,000 the Gregorian choir at St Chad's; he is shown on the bottom left in his choir cope, with lines of Gregorian chant notation. The enormous window is divided into pairs of ovals or vesicas on Marian themes: reading from bottom left, the Virgin as described in the Apocalypse, the creation of Eve and the expulsion from Paradise; and from bottom right the Annunciation, the Virgin Immaculate and the Coronation of the Virgin; between these two scenes can be seen Pope Pius IX defining the dogma of the Immaculate Conception in 1854. The flowing, fourteenth-century drawing style, the ethereal blues and reds, and the avoidance of the often cloying iconography of much nineteenth-century Marian piety make this one of Powell's most successful windows.[35]

The cathedral also possesses an important collection of vestments, such as the red cloth of gold vestments given by Lord Shrewsbury in 1841, the first of many such gifts,[36] a green cope by 'Mistress Powell and daughters', given by Pugin in 1841,[37] and a black cope and the Shrewsbury pall both designed by E. W. Pugin and J. H. Powell for Shrewsbury's funeral in 1852, made by the Misses Brown of Birmingham.[38]

E. W. Pugin added the upper sacristy in 1854, probably as part of the work to relocate the organ from the west end,[39] and in 1856 completed the second of the two spires.[40] Further additions are St Edward's Chapel (1933) on the north-west by Sebastian Pugin Powell,[41] with the story of the St Chad relics in the glass, and a confessional aisle to alleviate Pugin's inadequate provision.

After the disaster of the 1967–8 re-ordering, Archbishop Maurice Couve de Murville spent more than £2 million on the restoration of the church, using the architects Morgan Foster (to 1992) and then the Brownhill Duvall Partnership of Lichfield. A magnificent Walker organ in a towering neo-Gothic case by David Greabe has been placed at the west end, although its scale is without a Pugin precedent.[42] The new work reverses many of the mistakes of 1967–8 by Archbishop Dwyer, and it is certainly the most colourful restoration of a Pugin cathedral since that of Nottingham by F. A. Walters in 1926–7.[43]

1. See below.
2. BAA, B465, Pugin to John Hardman, 10 June 1837, referring to the 1837 scheme for a chapel, not the cathedral as built; Belcher (ed.), *Letters of Pugin*, I, pp. 77–8.
3. N. Pevsner, *South Lancashire* (Hardmonsworth, 1974), p. 331 (on Pugin's St Wilfrid's, Hulme, Manchester, 1839–41).
4. A. Wedgwood, (ed.), *Catalogue of the Drawings Collection of the RIBA, the Pugin Family* (1977), pp. 55–6.
5. Compare references in *Civil Engineer and Architects Journal*, II (1839), 477, and W. Greaney, *A Guide to St Chad's Cathedral Church, Bath Street, Birmingham* (Birmingham, 1877), pp. 32, 34.
6. Pugin's description in *Tablet* (1841), p. 398.
7. The Cathedral Clergy, *A History of St Chad's Cathedral, Birmingham, 1841–1904* (Birmingham, 1904), pp. 87, 147–50.
8. C. L. Eastlake, *History of the Gothic Revival* (1872), p. 162.
9. Ibid., pp. 156–7.
10. The major source for the furnishing and history of St Chad's are the two manuscripts BAA, P1/8/1 and 2, St Chad's Cathedral Records, I and II, on which subsequent guides are based.
11. Belcher (ed.), *Letters of Pugin*, I, pp. 153–7, 154.
12. *St Chad's Cathedral, 1841–1904*, pp. 80–1, 153.
13. Pugin to Phillipps, 18 December 1840, in Belcher (ed.), *Letters of Pugin*, I, pp. 174–5; see also Pugin to Shrewsbury, 5 January 1841, pp. 187–9; Pugin to Dr Rock, 13 December 1840, pp. 173–4; 2 February 1841, pp. 201–2; Pugin to Phillipps, 7 February 1841, pp. 206–7.
14. *The Golden Jubilee of St Chad's Cathedral Church* (Birmingham, 1891), p. 25; *A History of St Chad's Cathedral, 1841–1904*, p. 153. Two paintings, of St Augustine of Hippo and St Gregory, added to the screen survive in Cathedral House.
15. BAA, P1/8/1, f. 218; Belcher (ed.), *Letters of Pugin*, I, p. 148, note 8; C. Tracy, *Continental Church Furniture in England: A Traffic in Piety* (Woodbridge, 2002), pp. 188–9.
16. BAA, P1/8/1, f. 205; A. W. N. Pugin and B. Smith, *Glossary of Ecclesiastical Ornament and Costume* (1844), pp. 168–9; A. Wedgwood, 'A. W. Pugin's tours in Northern Europe', in J. de Maeyer and L. Verpoest (eds), *Gothic Revival: Religion, Architecture and Style in Western Europe 1815–1914* (KADOC-Artes, Leuven, 2000), pp. 92–8.
17. BAA, P1/8/1, f. 217; *Civil Engineer and Architects Journal*, II

(1839), p. 477; Tracy, *Continental Church Furniture*, pp. 224–6.

18. Belcher (ed.), *Letters of Pugin*, I, p. 175.

19. M. W. Greenslade, *St Chad of Lichfield and Birmingham* (Archdiocese of Birmingham Historical Commission, 1996).

20. The flanking angels and half-bust do not appear on the photograph of 1904; the Revd Dr John Sharp first noticed the discrepancy with the chest in the *c*.1910 photograph.

21. For Pugin's views on baldachins see Pugin and Smith, *Glossary*, pp. 72–5.

22. The gift of John Hardman junior, and the Powells: *Golden Jubilee of St Chad's Cathedral*, p. 25; they are sometimes confused with Pugin's gifts in 1841.

23. BAA, P1/8/1.

24. *St Chad's Cathedral, 1841–1904*, p. 154; recased by Brownhill Duval Partnership, 2001.

25. BAA, ADP/P1/17, plan of the re-ordering by Weigthman & Bullen; *The Victorian Society Annual Report, 1967–8*, pp. 6, 41–2; G. Stamp, 'Ambonoclasm redeemed', in *True Principles: The Voice of the Pugin Society*, Summer 2002.

26. Wedgwood, (ed.), *Catalogue of the Drawings Collection of the RIBA, the Pugin Family*, pp. 55–6.

27. Belcher (ed.), *Letters of Pugin*, I, pp. 160–1; *Tablet* (1841), pp. 397–8; S. Shepherd, 'Stained Glass', in Atterbury and Wainwright (eds), *Pugin*, pp. 195–6.

28. BAA, P1/8/1, f. 226; Pugin's description: *Tablet*, (1841), p. 398.

29. BAA, P1/8/1, f. 219; Greaney, *St Chad's*, p. 41.

30. Greaney, *St Chad's*, pp. 47–8, where 'E. W. Pugin' is a misprint for A. W. Pugin.

31. P. Spencer-Silver, *Pugin's Builder* (1993), pp. 4–5.

32. BAA, P1/8/1, ff. 212–15; Greaney, *St Chad's*, pp. 51–2.

33. Birmingham Central Library, Hardman Collection, Glass Order Day Book (1845–53), f. 100, 20 December 1853; *Golden Jubilee of St Chad's Cathedral*, p. 25, misdates it to 1865 (followed by M. Hodgetts, *St Chad's Cathedral, Birmingham*, Archdiocese of Birmingham Historical Commission, 1987, p. 12). For Hardman & Co at Dublin, *Builder*, 1853, p. 323; *Tablet*, 1853, p. 737.

34. See above, p. 14.

35. Greaney, *St Chad's*, pp. 56–62; *St Chad's Cathedral* (1904), pp. 97–105.

36. BAA, P1/8/1, f. 229; Belcher (ed.), *Letters of Pugin*, I, pp.

178-9 (note 4), pp. 80, 297-8; [R. O'Donnell], catalogue entry no. 55, in P. Atterbury (ed.), *A. W. N. Pugin: Master of the Gothic Revival* (New Haven and London, 1995), pp. 282-3.
37. BAA, P1/8/1, f. 230.
38. R. O'Donnell, 'No "maimed rites", The funeral obsequies of the Earl of Shrewsbury, 1852', in *True Principles: The Voice of the Pugin Society*, Summer 2002.
39. BAA, ADP/P1/12, E. W. Pugin drawing dated 1854 for sacristy.
40. *Golden Jubilee of St Chad's Cathedral*, p. 56.
41. Sebastian Pugin Powell (1866-1949), son of J. H. Powell, continued the Pugin & Pugin practice after P. P. Pugin's death in 1904.
42. Pugin gave an organ in 1844.
43. For Nottingham, see below.

BIRMINGHAM, THE BISHOP'S HOUSE

Pugin's Bishop's House (1840-1) was opposite the west front of the cathedral. It was demolished in the 1960s when the inner ring road was built.[1] Pugin illustrated and described the house in *Present State*.[2] Some of his contract drawings for his builder George Myers and Bishop Walsh, are in the Birmingham Archdiocesan Archives.[3] He seems to have given his designs free.[4] Its varied storey heights around a U-plan courtyard closed by a single storey wall show Pugin overturning Georgian building habits to evolve a part institutional, part domestic, part religious building, which he also explored in conventual architecture. Services were provided on the lower floors, a hall and chapel were on the first floor, and there was a taller residential wing. Historic photographs show that Pugin's apologetic entrance was replaced by a more emphatic High Victorian version. Bishop Ullathorne, the second occupant, understood the function of the great hall, where 'the table of the Bishop is open daily to all the clergy who come to visit him, ... so that they have no occasion to seek other *hospicium*'.[5]

1. A. Wedgwood, 'Domestic Architecture', in Atterbury and Wainwright (eds), *Pugin*, p. 51.
2. pp. 102–8, and pl. XI.
3. BAA, APD/P1/7–11, signed A. W. Pugin 1840, and Myers and Willson, builders.
4. Belcher (ed.), *Letters of Pugin*, I, p. 225.
5. Quotation from *Status Animarum* of Birmingham Diocese, 1856, quoted in D. A. Bellenger, *William Bernard Ullathorne* (Archdiocese of Birmingham Historical Commission, 2001), p. 15.

BIRMINGHAM, ST MARY'S COLLEGE, OSCOTT

Although Pugin's name is intimately associated with Oscott, he built very little here. His two gate lodges, through which visitors would have passed, are now isolated by the modern road entrances. From the great terrace looking down onto Birmingham, the ambitious range of brick and stone dressed Tudor Gothic buildings first known as New Oscott (1834–8) is revealed, not by Pugin but by Joseph Potter (*c.*1756–1842). He was the county surveyor of Staffordshire, architect to Lichfield Cathedral, and architect of the Catholic church at Newport, Shropshire (1832). Already a very old man, he was assisted by his sons Joseph and Robert, although their respective roles are complementary.[1] Pugin, who first arrived in 1837, dramatically took over from them the furnishing of the new chapel; although he is popularly supposed to have added the five-sided apse,[2] a close inspection shows that there are no breaks in the brickwork, and the evolution from straight-ended to apsed sanctuary was Potter's.[3] Pugin's first independent architectural work at Oscott was the Lady statue carved by Thomas Roddis and its niche on the terrace, perhaps also of 1837.[4] The attractive north and south lodges date from 1840 and are Pugin's only work here to be illustrated in the frontispiece to his *Apology for the Revival of Pointed or Christian Architecture* where the north lodge appears centrally in the foreground of the plate.[5] They are ably handled examples of his domestic architecture of the quality associated with his country-house, rather than church-building, commissions.

Pugin's most significant role at Oscott was not as architect but as antique dealer and decorator for the chapel. Fascinated by woodwork and joinery, he produced the extraordinary confection of the high altar, with antique fragments forming the triptych reredos sitting on a wooden substructure, the 'super-altar' of panelling and enamels, and the mensa and wooden frontal, all painted and gilded. The mensa was removed *c*.1968, but the painted frontal, identified in storage *c*.1983, is now refixed in place. Pugin also brought other antiques such as the Flemish baroque altar rails,[6] the stalls,[7] and the confessional, as well as moveable furnishings including metalwork, stained glass fragments and enamels. He also designed completely new furnishings, such as the prie-dieu.[8] All of this was anticipated in the etching of the chapel dated June 1837, which itself anticipated the consecration ceremonies of 29 May 1838.[9]

Otherwise, few Pugin drawings for Oscott survive, but one highly detailed design for the sanctuary shows him taking great pains with bosses on the theme of the Blessed Virgin's titles from the Litany of Loreto. Pugin was probably responsible too for the design of the figurative sculpture, executed by Thomas Roddis, all of it of high quality, especially the pulpit. This is reached up the stair in the bell turret, and, following medieval models, it is dramatically bracketed out of the wall. Could Newman actually have squeezed into it to deliver the 'Second Spring' sermon?[10] The stained glass of the apse (1837) was to Pugin's design, and incorporated medieval fragments. It was executed by William Warrington of London, whom Pugin sent to Rouen to study originals.[11] Another Warrington window at the head of the nave is to Pugin's design, but the rest of the glass is later, by J. H. Powell of Hardman & Co. By the early 1840s Pugin was much less at Oscott, and the painted stone altar and tabernacle with fine engraved metalwork dedicated to St George and St Patrick in the transept was supplied in 1842 and seems to have been his last major involvement with the chapel.[12] A rood screen was installed by Dr Weedall in 1846, as part of a Hardman & Co.

redecoration which occupied their painter John Earley for seventeen weeks; another redecoration followed in 1850, indicating the frequency of such campaigns in such heavily used buildings.[13]

In the sacristy Pugin installed many antique chests, including medieval pieces, which were well stocked with plate and vestments. The 16th Earl of Shrewsbury gave both antique vestments (the late medieval Waterford Cathedral set), the cloth of gold vestments made by Tyler & Lonsdale to Pugin's design for the opening, and many other vestments no longer surviving.[14] Much silver plate and base metalwork was supplied by Hardman & Co.[15] Pugin was also involved with the setting up and fitting out of the Museum housed in rooms off the chapel (now elsewhere),[16] and with the library, to which he presented copies of his books. But just as he complained of the state of his churches, he was horrified by the state of the library in 1841 and, significantly, none of his later books is in the collection.[17] He also furnished the professors' dining room, where an important series of portraits in Pugin frames and sets of dining chairs survive. The students' refectory has early Pugin tables and benches. The fireplace is topped by a later overmantel by E. W. Pugin.

Pugin produced designs for a chantry chapel to commemorate Bishop Milner in 1839,[18] but what was actually realized was only a ledger slab and brass to his design in 1841, one of his first collaborations with Hardman & Co. in this form.[19] Only in 1860 did E. W. Pugin extend the transept for chantry chapels, with further extensions later by P. P. Pugin, the whole known collectively as the Weedall chantry.[20] It houses the beautiful alabaster statue of the Virgin and Child, as *Sedes Sapientiae*, probably to the design of J. H. Powell, carved by Early and Powell of Dublin and said to have been shown at the 1862 London International Exhibition.[21] The elaborate painted setting of the memorial brasses on the wall behind is currently painted out.[22] The Pugins' last involvement was the Northcote Hall, designed by E. W. Pugin in 1859, begun in 1860 but completed to a lesser scheme (1878–9) by P. P. Pugin.[23]

1. R. O'Donnell, 'Pugin at Oscott', in Champ (ed.), *Oscott College, 1838–1988, a volume of commemorative essays* (1988), pp. 48–9, note 14.
2. W. Greaney, *The Buildings, Museum, Pictures, and Library at St Mary's College, Oscott* (Birmingham, 1899), p. 14; *The Oscotian*, 5, no. 1 (July 1905), p. 108.
3. R. O'Donnell, 'Pugin as a Church Architect' in Atterbury and Wainwright (eds.), *Pugin*, p. 79.
4. Thomas Roddis's name first appears in the Oscott accounts in 1835; he was paid the large sum of £14 'for carving and modelling the BVM statue' (Oscott archives, box 1837, receipts of Dr Weedall, 20 May 1837). He was also responsible for the architectural and figure carving of Pugin's lodges, and followed Pugin to Alton and Cheadle. He was a pupil of Sir Francis Chantrey (to whom the statue is sometimes wrongly attributed). See J. H. Thompson, 'A History of Oscott College', IV, *The Oscotian*, NS, vol I, no. 2 (1937), pp. 66, 72.
5. O'Donnell, 'Pugin at Oscott', in Champ (ed.), *Oscott College*, p. 55.
6. C. Tracy, *Continental Church Furniture in England: A Traffic in Piety* (Woodbridge, 2002), pp. 123–5.
7. Ibid., p. 267.
8. Based on that in Pugin's *Gothic Furniture of the Fifteenth Century* (1835), plate 1: O'Donnell, 'Pugin at Oscott', p. 53.
9. Ibid., pp. 50–2.
10. The unfinished painting by James Doyle, however, uses a certain artistic licence and groups the fathers of the Synod in the sanctuary and elsewhere.
11. Oscott Archives, box 1838, Warrington to Weedall, 18 July 1838. The glass is described in *OJ*, VI (1838), p. 90.
12. O'Donnell, 'Pugin at Oscott', p. 56, note 66.
13. Birmingham City Archives, Hardman Collection, Decoration Day Book (1846–50), payments to John Earley, 1 January 1846, p. 57.
14. O'Donnell, 'Pugin at Oscott', pp. 53–4, notes 47–9; Belcher (ed.), *Letters of Pugin*, I, pp. 87–9.
15. O'Donnell, 'Pugin at Oscott', pp. 57 (note), 88–9.
16. Ibid., pp. 58–9; Belcher (ed.), *Letters of Pugin*, I, pp. 116–18; Tracy, *Continental Church Furniture*, pp. 183–6.
17. O'Donnell, 'Pugin at Oscott', pp. 57–8; Belcher (ed.), *Letters of Pugin*, I, pp. 297–9.

18. *OJ*, VIII (1839), 402–3. Pugin's drawings survive at Oscott.
19. D. Meara, 'Monuments and Brasses', in Atterbury and Wainwright (eds), *Pugin*, pp. 188–9.
20. *Building News* (1860), p. 258; Greaney, *The Buildings, Museum, Pictures, and Library at St Mary's College, Oscott*, pp. 15–16.
21. Greaney, A Catalogue of Pictures ... (1880), p. 29; A. G. Well, 'Oscott Madonnas', *The Oscotian*, 1903, vol. 3 no. 3, p. 112 (reference Judith Champ). However, *The London International Exhibition, 1862, Official Catalogue, Fine Art* [and] *Catalogue, Industrial Department* do not identify it.
22. D. Meara, *Victorian Memorial Brasses* (1983), pp. 36–9, 50–5.
23. E. W. Pugin exhibited a design for this scheme at the Royal Academy in 1860: Wedgwood, *Catalogue of the Drawings Collection of the RIBA, the Pugin Family* (1977), p. 114, n. 11.

BIRMINGHAM, THE MERCY CONVENT, HANDSWORTH

Handsworth is now a poor inner city limbo. In the nineteenth cetnury it was a mixture of suburban villas, market gardens, and poor cottages. A villa in the Gothic style was John Hardman senior's house; with the addition of a Puginesque porch it is now the presbytery of St Francis' Church (1894).[1] Opposite, in the late 1830s John Hardman acquired a site for the first Mercy Convent in the Midlands, which he founded in 1840. The Earl of Shrewsbury gave £2,000, and Hardman gave the buildings and furnishings which cost £5,535;[2] he also gave his daughter, who as Mother Mary Juliana Hardman (1813–84) was one of the first nuns and eventually Mother Superior.[3]

Pugin's romantic Catholicism identified strongly with the revival of the religious orders, and he had definite views on the necessity of a strict enclosure required by the rules of orders of monks and nuns founded in the Middle Ages. But the Mercy Sisters' active apostolate did not require an enclosure. Pugin, so adept in recreating medieval buildings, made some of his best convents for the distinctly 'modern' Sisters of Mercy, recently founded in Dublin, and he built their first

English convent at Bermondsey (1839–40).[4] Pugin's work there was criticized by the foundress of the Order, Catherine McAuley (1778–1841), who wrote to Bishop Walsh in 1840: 'the sleeping rooms are too large, the corridors confined and not well lighted, and all the Gothic work made it expensive.'[5] At Handsworth Catherine McCauley was able to give clear directions on the plan required, telling Dr Walsh: 'I am not so afraid of Mr Pugin as I was, he is so fond of high walls and few windows.'[6] When she finally saw Handsworth she was converted, describing it as 'this beautiful convent erected by Mr Pugin in the ancient monastic style', and recommended it in 1841 as a model for another convent to the Bishop of Galway.[7]

The family association is underlined in the portrait of John Hardman senior,[8] now at the convent, in which the convent chapel forms the background; on his death, as was the pious custom, the nuns took in his widow, who spent twenty-six years here.[9] There are also the charming bird's-eye views by his sixteen-year-old nephew, J. H. Powell, entitled 'General prospect of Hardman's Hospital',[10] based on Pugin's bird's-eye drawing published in *Present State*.[11] These drawings expressed the idealized world of medieval Catholic charity which Pugin had evoked in *Contrasts*, and built at Alton Hospital. A memorandum addressed to Hardman emphasized, as Pugin did so often, the economy of the construction, such as the timber partitions and roof forms, and the absence of mouldings, claiming that 'you will perceive I have studied the greatest economy'. This was obviously meant to be read in conjunction with Pugin's drawings and was also addressed to George Myers.[12]

The original buildings of red brick with blue-brick and stone dressings, and prominent slate roofs, said to be based on Brown's Hospital in Stamford, consisted of two intersecting ranges forming an L-plan. The main range with its gable-end is onto Hunter's Lane, and its three-storey massing and externally expressed staircase arrangement remind us of Pugin experimenting in the same mode at his first house, St Marie's Grange, Salisbury.[13] At right angles is the range fronting the cloister quadrangle, the two other arms of which form a charmingly scaled cloister. Another arm extends to the road, with a porch forming 'the almonry for the daily relief of the poor'.[14] The sanctuary of the chapel was damaged by bombing during the Second World War and rebuilt on a larger scale.[15] The small stalled chapel was on an east–west axis with the refectory range and its fittings were excluded from the memorandum to Hardman. A letter from Pugin to Herbert Minton of 19 September 1840 suggests that the tiled floor here was to be their first collaboration.[16] Above the refectory and the ante-chapel were cells for the nuns.[17] Pugin took great pains to furnish the interior; he wrote to J. R. Bloxam: 'I am erecting a hospital for the sisters of charity [*sic*] at Birmingham. It is quite in the solemn devotional spirit of Catholic England. no French dolls. "No tinsel or Milliners finery" are to be found within its walls.'[18] Instead, Pugin installed medieval carvings, especially in the cloisters, which today jostle with the very *bondieuseries* he denounced. Some of the refectory furniture has been sold, but the rather incongruous grandfather clock survives.[19] There is a later three-storey addition of the 1850s at the south.[20] A second cloister and church were added in 1846–7.[21] The double aisle plan (one for the nuns, the other for the laity, following medieval precedent) embraced the tower and housed over four hundred. Both it and the 'house of mercy or refuge for unemployed servant girls' (1844)[22] were demolished after the war damage.

1. Belcher (ed.), *Letters of Pugin*, I, pp. 398–9. It was awarded an English Heritage blue plaque in 2002, commemorating John Hardman junior.
2. Greaney, *St. Chad's*, pp. 24–6, 151–8.
3. Gillow, *Dictionary*, III, pp. 128–33, see Mother Mary Juliana Hardman; [by a member of the Order of Mercy] *Leaves from the Annals of the Sisters of Mercy, II, England and the Colonies* (New York, 1883), pp. 309–16.
4. *Catholic Directory* (1840), pp. 96–9.
5. Sister Angela M. Bolster, *The Correspondence of Catherine McAuley, 1827–1841* (Cork, 1989), pp. 120–1.
6. Ibid., pp. 147–8; *Leaves from the Annals, II*, pp. 341–2.

7. *Leaves from the Annals*, II, pp. 371–2.
8. It is mistakenly identified in Atterbury and Wainwright (eds), *Pugin*, p. 175, as 'John Hardman junior'.
9. *Leaves from the Annals, II*, pp. 314–16.
10. Of the eight drawings in the convent archives, dated 1841, only one, the 'general prospect', is signed by J. H. Powell: information from Sr Mary Barbara, 11 December 2001.
11. pp. 108–10, and plate XII.
12. This undated document, not in Pugin's hand, is labelled 'Mr Pugin's instructions for the building of the Convent to Mr Myers for him to make out particulars and to estimate . . .': Handsworth Mercy Convent Archives (courtesy of Sr Mary Barbara); Belcher (ed.), *Letters of Pugin*, I, p. 140.
13. *Civil Engineer and Architects Journal*, III (1840), 215; *OJ*, X (1840), 351–2; XI, 125.
14. Pugin, *Present State*, pp. 108–10; Belcher (ed.), *Letters of Pugin*, I, pp. 398–9.
15. The stalls from the choir are now in St Francis's Church: information from Sr Mary Barbara, 11 December 2001.
16. Information from the Revd M. Fisher; Pugin, *Present State* (1843), p. 73.
17. There are frequent references to the furnishing and decoration of the convent and church in the Birmingham City Archives, Hardman Collection, Decoration Day Book (1845–50), and Glass Day Book (1845–53). See also Greaney, *St Chad's*, pp. 24–6.
18. Belcher (ed.), *Letters of Pugin*, I, pp. 140–1.
19. For the former state of the refectory see R. O'Donnell, 'Pugin as a Church Architect', in Atterbury and Wainwright (eds), *Pugin*, p. 82, plate 151.
20. *Leaves from the Annals*, II, pp. 347–52.
21. *Builder* (1846), p. 189; (1847), p. 245.
22. Greaney, *St Chad's*, pp. 25–6.

BIRMINGHAM, ST. JOSEPH, NECHELLS

Pugin built the chancel and Lady Chapel of an intended church for the Birmingham Catholic cemetery, with which the Hardmans were also associated, in 1850.[1] The original chapel, of sandstone ashlar with slate roofs, was a carefully considered work. Internally it is two bays long with an arcade between the two spaces. Pugin's Lady altar and tabernacle survive, as does his high altar, with its very rare painted wooden frontal, hung from hooks. The wooden reredos, painted and gilt, is dated 1902; it has a fine marble and bas-relief silver tabernacle door, typical of Birmingham fine metalwork of this date. E. W. Pugin added two parallel naves (1872) in red and blue brick with stone dressings and slate roofs.[2] Internally he made two arches to the chapel and chancel. His extraordinary bold pier-capitals and roof survive, but those by A. W. Pugin at the east end were replaced after 1945 by Sir Giles Scott, who added the reredos to the Lady Chapel, the benches and the doors. The excellent Stations of the Cross, in a late fourteenth-century Flemish style, are examples of the high quality work exported from Belgium in the second half of the nineteenth century and are much influenced by Pugin; they are in their original frames. There is Hardman glass from 1849 onwards. E. W. Pugin also designed the adjacent priest's house and a school.

1. *Tablet* (1850), p. 612.
2. *Building News* (1872), p. 342; *Architect* (1874), p. 118; W. Greaney, *A Guide to St Chad's Cathedral* (Birmingham, 1877), pp. 28–9; *Victoria County History of Warwickshire*, VII, p. 408.

BREWOOD, ST MARY

This church and brick presbytery, school and schoolhouse in Staffordshire make a highly attractive group. Built in 1843–4, St Mary's is an example of the rural village church which so fascinated romantic religious minds in the 1840s. Pugin wrote enthusiastically to Lord Shrewsbury: 'The church can stand due east and west with a south porch to the road, and a church in such a situation for an old Catholic population is most interesting.'[1] Its red sandstone and squat proportions reflect the 'natural', picturesque impulse behind much of Pugin's architecture. It has a west tower with broach spire, a nave with no clerestory and aisles of low head height, and a sacristy on the north side. There is a porch and an external door in the easternmost bay of the south aisle; the deep squint between it and the chancel is expressed externally as a substantial kink in the wall. Was this to provide a separate access and view of the altar for the last Catholic member of the Giffard family, who had paid for the site?

The church, which cost £1,345, was consecrated in June 1844.[2] The first four bays have octagonal piers; the fifth pier is squared off to mark a screen and rood loft, now missing. They support tall arches, echoing the satisfying proportions of the exterior. There is a tall tower arch. The gradual elaboration of the three different roof forms define the different status of each part of the church, from the simple lean-to rafters of the aisles, the nave with principals on stone corbels, to the chancel with close-set scissors springing from principals supported on corbels. Three stained glass windows were Pugin's gift. Still in position is the font of remarkably abstract design, which could be mistaken for the work of the Anglican architect William Butterfield ten years later: rising from a boldly chamfered base is a simple bowl with a floriated cross and Lamb of God roundel its only decoration. It must be from George Myers's workshop.[3] The Pugin altar survives on a five-step platform with deep-set quatrefoils in the mensa and in the stone reredos. For this small mission there is a single sedile for the single celebrant (rather than the three-seat sedilia for High Mass) and a piscina. The Lady Chapel has a Wailes window and a Minton floor. The 1914–18 war memorial window reflects the conservatism of Hardman & Co.'s work by that date. The priest founder, Robert Richmond, who died in 1844, is commemorated in a monument and brass by Pugin in the chancel,[4] as is his nephew William Richmond, who succeeded as priest and died in 1848.[5] Myers was also builder of the presbytery, school and schoolhouse, making his total bill £2,010.[6]

The need for a church in this rural setting is explained by the long established historic recusant missions of Blackladies and Longbirch, which Brewood superseded. On Census Sunday in 1851 there was a thriving congregation of 400 at

Mass and 270 at the afternoon service, probably Vespers or Benediction.[7]

1. House of Lords Record Office 339/26 Pugin to Shrewsbury, *c*.1843, (ref. supplied by the Revd M. Fisher).
2. *Tablet* (1844), p. 390.
3. Photograph from Brian Andrews, 2001, and comments by the Revd M. Fisher.
4. BAA, P99/8/48, letter William Richmond to George Richmond, 15 September 1844 (ref. supplied by the Revd J. Sharp).
5. F. C. Husenbeth, 'Robert, William and Henry Richmond' in *Staffordshire Catholic History*, 19 (1980), pp. 12–27 (ref. supplied by M. Greenslade).
6. P. Spencer-Silver, *Pugin's Builder* (1993), p. 251.
7. *Victoria County History of Staffordshire*, V, 45.

BRIERLEY HILL, ST MARY

E. W. Pugin's church (1872–3), consists of nave, and sanctuary, aisle and side chapel.[1]

1. *Building News* (1872), p. 489; 1873, p. 471; *Tablet* (1875) pp. 530–1.

BROMSGROVE, ST PETER

The church of St Peter (1862), by Gilbert Blount,[1] houses the Alton Towers high altar. Bromsgrove had been a mission centred on the fifteenth-century Grafton Manor, a property of the Talbot family, and the 16th Earl of Shrewsbury was born here. Pugin made designs for furnishing the medieval domestic chapel in 1850.[2] This was lost to the local Catholics in 1856, but the altar continued the Shrewsbury connection. He wrote of 'the altar etc. entirely finished'[3] in a letter of 1839, but we know little about its genesis, or for example the artist of the *ex dono* paintings of the Earl and Countess, behind whom can be seen details of Alton Towers, in the reredos.[4]

1. N. Pevnser, *Worcestershire* (Harmondsworth, 1968), p. 157.
2. Pugin's Diary, 1850, end papers [c], p. 70 and decoration by Crace & Co., nos. 307–8, in Wedgwood, *Pugin Family*, pp. 70, 94–5. Pugin's letters are at the RIBA: A. Wedgwood, *Catalogue of the Drawings Collection of the RIBA, the Pugin Family* (1977), pp. 109–11.
3. Belcher (ed.), *Letters of Pugin*, I, p. 115; the corresponding charges in the Hardman archive (ibid. p. 116) are for 1840.
4. R. O'Donnell, 'Pugin as a Church Architect', in Atterbury and Wainwright (eds), *Pugin*, p. 68, plate 121. It was included in the exhibition 'Pugin, a Gothic Passion' at the Victoria & Albert Museum in 1994.

CHEADLE, ST GILES

Cheadle is a place where, for once, the triumphantly spired Catholic church of St Giles (1840–6) dominates the town, especially the humble Anglican church, also St Giles (1837–9), by the local architect J. P. Pritchett. Cheadle is Pugin's most elaborate church, built in local red stone from the Counslow quarry on the Alton estate. Pugin designed the church in 1840, but only a single drawing, showing the elaborate details of the pulpit and Easter Sepulchre, survives. He wrote to Lord Shrewsbury in 1841 that he was to employ only 'your Lordsips [*sic*] own stone timber & men',[1] and Shrewsbury's 'man' John Denny was clerk of works. The beautifully cut ashlar stone has much architectural, heraldic and inconographic carving by Thomas Roddis (who died in 1845); some figure sculpture is actually ochre sandstone painted red. The steeply-pitched roofs are covered in lead, with cast-iron crestings; the materials are of the most expensive. The church has a west tower, north and south porches, a five-bay nave and aisles and two side chapels, the Blessed Sacrament chapel on the south, the Lady Chapel on the north. The two-bay chancel projects beyond. The ensemble of west door, tower and spire especially could be a plate from a contemporary Gothic Revival textbook. Pugin claimed that the church's lavishness and proportions became possible due to additional funding after the building was begun, but he invariably proposed elaborate spires (at Southwark and Newcastle neither was completed by him); he clearly planned such a work from foundation upwards, although the detail is more elaborate than as originally published. The planning and liturgical provision also became more and more elaborate: the plan published in *Present State* in 1841 was soon out of date.[2] Although Cheadle was first described by Pugin in 1841 as 'though small & simple it will be a perfect revival',[3] and 'not by any means a rich building. It is a simple country parish church',[4] it was to become through its furnishing and decoration Pugin's most splendid church and was to serve 'as a model . . . an opportunity of showing the real revival',[5] which 'will be seen by thousands'.[6]

Shrewsbury bought this prominent site in 1837 and cleared it for the church and for the churchyard to be defined by walls and gates. Pugin was very precise about its positioning: 'The church stands exactly as it ought to do, the Tower within a few feet of the street fronting the market place.'[7] In front of the tower is a stone Crucifixion, and at the (ritual) south-east is the two-storey primary school (1841–6). The former convent of St Joseph, a building dating from the eighteenth century, was adapted by Pugin in 1848–9 to form a three-sided plan, with a single-storey cloister on the churchyard side and a two-storey domestic range and gabled tower.[8] Pugin also built a presbytery on Charles Street, since sold off.

Pugin obviously delighted in the rich building materials of the church and varied his details, such as the depth of the buttresses, and particularly the window tracery, as much as he could, making his often-repeated claim that each window was different. The prominent site allowed him carefully to express the different functions of each part: the multi-gabled group on the north side is made up of the single-storey outer sacristy and porch, with the stair-tower to the organ loft appearing above and the inner sacristy below. This he defended against Shrewsbury's desire for a west organ gallery.[9] A similar part-domestic, part-religious range occurs at Ramsgate, where it may have been intended as the lodging of the priest. Another staircase, emphasized externally as a multi-sided projection, gives access to the pulpit and rood loft within the thickness of the chancel arch. Pugin also delighted in the grouping of the different roof forms, particularly that of the chancel, the Lady Chapel, and the Blessed Sacrament chapel, an elaboration suggested by Lord Shrewsbury. The two nave porches have stone tiled roofs and are vaulted.

Entering the church, either through a porch or the west door, is like opening a medieval Book of Hours: light floods through the clear-glazed west window and massive tower arch (where Shrewsbury had talked of a gallery) and through the stained glass. This is truly a building meant to be explored, as one 'reads' the plan, the spaces, and the elaborate iconography and texts. The proportions are low, the light filtered, the roofs heavy in effect; the aisles with lean-to purlin roofs, the nave with wall posts supporting 'open' trusses with pierced tracery at the apex, all these members are painted. The arcades, with capitals cut by Roddis, which Pugin thought were 'by far the best thing done since the old time and every one different',[10] are stone but painted, with the walls plastered and painted with stencils. Each corner of the church is heavily furnished in wood, metalwork or stone. The decorative artists involved were 'men I have ... schooled',[11] as Pugin put it; the architectural sculpture was by Roddis and the later carving in stone, alabaster and wood was probably by George Myers's London men. The overall internal polychromatic painting was probably by Thomas Kearns[12] but the prophets (nave), kings (tower inner face), angels (sanctuary) on zinc roundels and the Blessed Sacrament chapel are to surviving Pugin sketches by Crace & Co.[13] A Herr Hauser painted the Last Judgement on canvas over the chancel arch and the Man of Sorrows on metal in the Easter Sepulchre.[14] Pugin fought hard to defend his increasing elaboration of decoration, and described interiors seen during a tour of Norfolk in 1844: 'I have seen such churches with the *painting and gilding nearly perfect!!!* ... I shall have glorious authorities at Cheadle',[15] but he later regretted the over-intensity of the painted decoration, and for his own church at Ramsgate he left the ashlar-finished walls unpainted. All the stained glass was by William Wailes of Newcastle with whom Pugin was in collaboration c.1841–5.[16] Herbert Minton, who revived the medieval encaustic floor tile-making techniques, reproduced them to Pugin's exacting heraldic, iconographic and text designs; they were laid down in 1844.[17] The fixed metalwork, such as the brass and wrought-iron screens to the baptistery and the Blessed Sacrament chapel and the west doors with the Talbot lions, are all by Hardman & Co., who were also responsible for the moveable metalwork and the sacristy and altar metalwork, all supplied in a great rush for the opening on 1 September 1846.[18] The elm benches in the nave were ready at this time; the aisle benches are later and obscure the stone wall-seats.

Each separate liturgical area received particular attention. The baptistery has a painted and gilt alabaster font under a wooden spired cover. The Wailes window has the obscure iconography of eight gifts associated with baptism, identified as 'largitas, humilitas, pietas, misericordia, modestia, patientia, pudicitia'.[19] The Blessed Sacrament chapel behind its exquisite brass screen has an altar of alabaster with paint and gilding. There is an elaborately carved panelled stone pulpit for which a drawing survives.[20] Pugin supplied a notable antique late-fifteenth-century triptych in carved wood for the Lady Chapel. The climax is the rood screen of oak, made on the Alton estate as early as 1842.[21] It is painted and gilt, with its loft and rood group of Our Lady and St John flanking the Crucifixion. Within the sanctuary are further elaborate provisions for a medieval liturgy: sedilia for three priests and a piscina, the Easter Sepulchre (based on the tomb of Aylmer de Valence in Westminster Abbey) and the high altar of alabaster, painted and gilt. The reredos is completely detached from the altar and at first there was to be a fixed tabernacle here, but the crucifix, a 'richly gilt cross and figure set with crystals and enamels for high altar ... £34.10s.' which rises from a shaft so as to fit behind 'one iron tabernacle with richly gilt plated inlaid ... enamel border set with crystal ... £75' were both delivered on 22 August 1846.[22] The Blessed Sacrament was reserved in its own chapel, reached through an arch, but the clergy invariably moved tabernacles to the high altars and made such chapels into Sacred Heart shrines, so that Pugin's liturgical point was lost. The chapel is vaulted, and decorated with vines, leaves, chalice and host iconography. The window has the Risen Christ in the stained glass with the text 'Amen, Amen dico vobis ego sum panis vivus [qui] de caelo descendit', which Pugin preferred to the ubiquitous Sacred Heart. However, windows to the Immaculate Heart of Mary and the Sacred Heart do appear in the south aisle, no doubt much to Pugin's chagrin, since he disapproved of such 'modern' devotions. The church was lavishly fitted with base and precious metalwork for its opening.[23] Like St Chad's, St Giles has always been recognized as of singular importance, and its screen and sanctuary survive unaltered.[24]

1. Belcher (ed.), *Letters of Pugin*, I, p. 293.
2. p. 16, plate I. Pugin's enthusiasm for the church can be followed in letters to Shrewsbury in Wedgwood, *Pugin Family*, pp. 102–9.
3. Belcher (ed.), *Letters of Pugin*, I, p. 186.
4. Ibid., p. 194.
5. Ibid., p. 335.
6. Ibid., p. 250.
7. Ibid., p. 250.
8. *Leaves from the Annals of the Sisters of Mercy, II, England and the Colonies* (New York, 1883), pp. 471–2. The nuns left after 1856.
9. Belcher (ed.), *Letters of Pugin*, I, pp. 269, 328–9.
10. Ibid., p. 297.
11. Magdalen College, Oxford, Archives: Bloxam MS no. 53, Pugin to J. R. Bloxam, 24 December 1850.
12. 'Mr Kearns, his Lordship's painter to whom the church at Cheadle owes its exquisite ... finishes': *Illustrated London News* (1852), p. 563. He died in 1856.
13. Wedgwood, *Pugin Family*, p. 187, nos. 248–50.
14. Probably Eduard Caspar Hauser (1807–1864), a Swiss pupil of Overbeck: E. Bénézit, *Dictionnaire ... des Peintres* (1966 edn), 4, p. 613.
15. Wedgwood, *Pugin Family*, p. 108.
16. Shepherd, 'Stained glass', in Atterbury and Wainwright (eds), *Pugin*, pp. 197–200.

17. Wedgwood, *Pugin Family*, p. 109. P. Atterbury, 'Ceramics', in Atterbury and Wainwright (eds), *Pugin*, pp. 143–52.
18. Birmingham City Archives, Hardman Collection, Metalwork Day Book (1846–June 1848), *passim*.
19. Brian Andrews comments: 'There is a whole book to be written on Cheadle as a theological textbook' (letter to the author, 3 September 2000).
20. A. Wedgwood, *The Catalogue of the Drawings Collection of the RIBA, the Pugin Family* (1977), no. [40], p. 57 and fig. 70.
21. Belcher (ed.), *Letters of Pugin*, I, pp. 325–6.
22. Birmingham City Archives, Hardman Collection, Metalwork Day Book (1845–June 1848) 'no 74' 22 August 1846; [R. O'Donnell], catalogue entries 'Ecclesiastical work', no. 64, p. 295, in Atterbury (ed.), *Pugin, Master of the Gothic Revival* (1995).
23. [R. O'Donnell] catalogue entries 'Ecclesiastical work', nos. 55–72, 74–76, and 82, in Atterbury (ed.), *Pugin, Master of the Gothic Revival* (1995).
24. Higham and Carson, *Pugin's Churches of the Second Spring;* W. G. Short, *The story of Cheadle Church, Staffordshire* (1969); Short, *Pugin's Gem – a brief history of the Catholic Church of St Giles, Cheadle, Staffordshire* (1981).

COTTON, ST WILFRID

The church of St Wilfrid, Cotton, now serves only local Catholics; until 1987 Cotton College, the continuance of the historical Sedgley Park School, was here.[1] Its beautiful site and the small eighteenth-century country house were given by Shrewsbury to the followers of Fr F. W. Faber, who shared with him the cost of building the church of St Wilfrid (1846–8).[2] The style is Gothic of *c*.1300, and the stonework is randomly coursed and with irregularly sized blocks particularly as quoin-work, all under blue fish-scale pattern tiled roofs. The plan is a broad nave with a south aisle under a separately hipped roof and south-west tower and spire. It has a three-light nave and aisle windows, a four-light west window over the door, a large north sacristy and a stone cloister to the Hall. The east end was lengthened and rebuilt in 1936–7 by George Drysdale. The three-light

Blessed Virgin window (with kneeling Fr Faber and St Peter) is by Pugin and Hardman and has been reset; there is reset glass in the west window; there is a *c*.1880 window, much 1930s Hardman & Co. glass, and two painted reredoses by J. Alphege Pippet.[3] Pugin's wish for a rood screen was rejected, and the form and size of the altar and tabernacle installed by Faber in 1848 were disputed by Pugin. On a visit with Phillipps in May 1848 Pugin had his first contretemps with Faber, who affected Italian styles of devotion and referred to the Blessed Virgin as 'Mama': this was to be the opening salvo in the Rood Screen Controversy.[4] Pugin designed a seated statue of the Virgin under a stone canopy for the terrace, which was moved to the church of St Thomas More, Coventry, when the school closed.[5] In 1846–8 Pugin added a right or north-east wing to Cotton Hall. Faber left after two years, and Shrewsbury's support for the Catholic establishment of Cotton Hall is therefore an example of the sort of over-generous provision of facilities criticized by George Montgomery, the Black Country priest, as being of no benefit to the struggling town congregations. Faber and his followers were succeeded by the Passionists, and then by Cotton College, for which a left wing (1874–5) was added, probably by the builder George Heveningham, who, E. W. Pugin claimed, pirated designs that he had made in 1866 for extensive buildings to house 200 boys.[6] This was part of E. W. Pugin's wider dispute with Bishop Ullathorne, and the tone of the exchanges is evidence of his persecution mania.

1. F. Roberts and N. Henshaw, *A History of Sedgley Park and Cotton College* (Preston, 1985).
2. Ward, *Sequel*, II, pp. 254–5; R. Addington, *Faber, Poet and Priest* (1974), pp. 149–50.
3. Higham and Carson, *Pugin's Churches*, pp. 59–69.
4. Addington, *Faber*, pp. 177–9; Purcell, *Phillipps*, I, pp. 212–13, 216–17, 219–22; II, pp. 208–9.
5. It was moved by the last priest-headmaster, Mgr Thomas Gavin.
6. BAA, SC/C3/1–8, E. W. Pugin to Canon Moore, February 1866, and to Canon Souter 29 April and 18 May 1874. George Heveningham was an old boy of Sedgley Park: Roberts and Henshaw, *A History of Cotton College*, p. 122.

DERBY, ST MARY

The scale and character of St Mary, Derby (1838–9), makes it the first of Pugin's churches to challenge that of contemporary state-funded Anglican church-building, especially the 'Commissioners' Churches' which he caricatured in *Contrasts*. At Derby Pugin made a specific challenge, or perhaps homage, with his tower to the early sixteenth-century tower of the nearby All Saints (the body of which was rebuilt by Gibbs in 1725), prompting the snide comment from B. F. L. Clarke: 'It is a common failing of the English Romanists to represent their geese as swans ... All Saints ... is a magnificent renaissance swan; and St Marie's ... is but a Gothic goose'.[1] Visual comparison can however no longer be made as the relationship has been destroyed by the chasm of a ring road so that the church is approached from the town across a concrete footbridge. Ancillary buildings such as the presbytery shown in the fund raising prints and in Pugin's 1837 presentation drawings have also been demolished.[2]

This was Pugin's most important Perpendicular style church, with a slender 'west' tower (it is not orientated east–west as a hostile review in the High Church Anglican magazine, the *British Critic* pointed out),[3] a five-bay nave and lean-to roofed aisles, and an apsed sanctuary. The nave arcades with their four-centred arches are of startlingly slight and high proportions and have a close-set clerestory above; the roof is supported on wall posts and elaborate tracery-detailed trusses.[4] The chancel arch has within it a subsidiary Gothic arch of timber supporting the rood and figures, but there was no screen below. The sanctuary is an apse, with large windows. It was the first large-scale building on which Pugin and his new-found builder George Myers collaborated, at a cost of £8,027.[5]

The priest, the unusually energetic and ambitious Thomas Sing (1808–1882),[6] was one of Pugin's early clerical supporters in the Midlands, although Pugin was complaining two years later of his use of the church and that he had 'marbled his ceilings and filled the rectory with the vilest assortment that vulgarity could combine'.[7] The dedication in October 1839 saw one of the set-piece contretemps between Pugin and the officiating clergy over the substitution of an orchestral Mass setting for the expected plain chant, so Pugin, Phillips and Lord Shrewsbury departed before the ceremony began, taking their cloth of gold Gothic vestments with them.[8] But the real significance of the church was noted instead by Wiseman, who hailed it as 'the real transition from chapel to church architecture amongst us',[9] and 'it would not have done dishonour to Rome'.[10] The already large church was extended and refurnished in 1855 by E. W. Pugin, who added a Pieta chapel at the end of the epistle aisle, and a much larger 'daily' chapel and sacristies beyond the line of the apse. In contrast to his father's Perpendicular, the extensions are Decorated. In what must have been one of the first such replacements, he substituted for his father's wooden altar and triptych a Caen stone and marble altar and reredos, with appropriate metalwork.[11] He also inserted a wrought-iron and brass screen below the rood – at £250, the most expensive metalwork order of that year at Hardman & Co.[12] – and a metalwork pulpit,[13] both since removed. A Minton & Co. floor was laid down, and painted decoration was carried out 'to the design of E. W. Pugin assisted by J. Powell, who is also the designer of the glass',[14] replacing the three earlier apse windows by Warrington with new ones, but still to Perpendicular design on the Tree of Jesse theme.[15] The glass and sculptural group in the Pieta chapel were by J. H. Powell[16] and further metalwork railings and gates were added. The church was redecorated again in 1892[17] and in the 1930s.[18] The most recent re-ordering (*c*.1984) was by Gerald Goalen & Partner.

1. B. F. L. Clarke, *Church Builders of the Nineteenth Century* (1938), p. 62.
2. Stanton, *Pugin*, pp. 43–7.
3. Belcher (ed.), *Letters of Pugin*, I, pp. 153–8.
4. A. Wedgwood, *Catalogue of the Drawings Collection of the RIBA, the Pugin Family* (1977), p. 57.
5. Spencer-Silver, *Pugin's Builder*, p. 239.

6. Belcher (ed.), *Letters of Pugin*, I, pp. 80–1.
7. Ibid., pp. 297–9.
8. Ward, *Sequel*, I, pp. 115–16; Belcher (ed.), *Letters of Pugin*, I, pp. 125–6; Purcell, *Phillipps*, II, pp. 222–4. Shrewsbury also gave vestments for this church.
9. Nicholas Wiseman in *Dublin Review* (1839), pp. 240–71, quote p. 244.
10. Ward, *Life and Times of Cardinal Wiseman*, I, pp. 310, 314–19.
11. Birmingham City Archives, Hardman Collection, Metalwork Day Book (Dec. 1854–Dec. 1857), f. 115, 28 June 1855, altar fittings etc. £30 10s; f. 129, 26 July 1855, altar garniture, including 'big six' etc., £59 1s 6d.
12. Ibid., f. 110, 18 June 1855.
13. Ibid., f. 160, 4 October 1855, £47 10s.
14. *Builder* (1855), p. 513.
15. Birmingham City Archives, Hardman Collection, Glass Book 1852–6, 27 January 1854. This is mistaken for the Warrington glass by A. Wedgwood in P. Howell and I. Sutton (eds), *The Faber Guide to Victorian Churches* (1989), p. 32.
16. *Builder* (1855), p. 513; Birmingham City Archives, Hardman Collection, Glass Book 1852–6, 13 November 1854; ibid., Metal Book (1854–57), f. 308, 1 October 1854, at £75.
17. *Tablet* (1892), p. 837.
18. M. Trappes Lomax, *Pugin, a Medieval Victorian* (1932), pp. 101–2.

DUDLEY, OUR BLESSED LADY AND ST THOMAS OF CANTERBURY

The Hon. and Revd George Spencer[1], who bought the site in 1837,[2] was the patron for two designs, the first of October 1838 for an apsed church (related to the St Chad's Cathedral scheme)[3] and the second for the church as built in 1839–40 in the Early English style.[4] Pugin condemned a description of it in the *Tablet* as 'written by some Irishman as a greater tissue of absurdities I never saw in so small a compass'.[5] It is a large church, with a five-bay nave with clerestory, lean-to aisles, and a single-bay sanctuary and Lady Chapel. Pugin described the church in *Present State*,[6] dwelling as usual on the furnishings, but his earlier comment to Phillipps, that 'Dudley is a compleat facsimile of one of the old English parish churches and nobody seems to know how to use it',[7] anticipated the disputes that he was to have with the clergy that culminated in the Rood Screen Controversy. Despite this, and early criticism of its screen,[8] Pugin attended the consecration on Easter Tuesday 1842.[9] In the 1960s Pugin's sacristies were replaced by another chapel and flat-roofed extensions which mar the elevations. The fittings have all been stripped out and only the font survives.[10] Pugin's 'open' roof has been low ceiled. Some stained glass by Warrington, Wailes and Hardman[11] has been reset in clear fields.

1. George Spencer (1799–1864) was priest at West Bromwich.
2. B. Kelly, *English Catholic Missions* (1907), p. 158.
3. Pugin's October 1838 drawings are at the Yale Centre for British Art, New Haven, Connecticut.
4. *Tablet* (1841), p. 22.
5. Belcher (ed), *Letters of Pugin*, I, p. 192.
6. pp. 33–4, 42, 63 and plate VII.
7. Purcell, *Phillipps*, II, pp. 213–15; Belcher (ed.), *Letters of Pugin*, I, pp. 174–6; Pugin's Diary, 29 March 1842, in Wedgwood, *Pugin Family*, pp. 51, 87.
8. Belcher (ed.), *Letters of Pugin*, I, pp. 201–2.
9. *Tablet* (1842), p. 247; *OJ*, XIV (1842), p. 269.
10. *Church of Our Lady and St Thomas of Canterbury, Dudley* (1965); no architect's name is given.
11. *Builder* (1867), p. 103.

GARENDON PARK

In 1862 Ambrose Phillipps inherited Garendon Hall, Leicestershire, an eighteenth-century Palladian house.[1] Pugin had made elaborate designs for a Gothic Garendon in 1841, almost an 'ideal' scheme, which remained on paper.[2] Pugin usually altered or decorated country houses, but we can see how he would have liked to build them in his drawings for Garendon and in the plate 'Old English Catholic Mansion' in

True Principles.[3] Quite what Phillipps asked for is not clear; he seems to have been presented with a fait-accompli bird's-eye scheme, of the type that Pugin gave to other astonished patrons, such as the monks of Downside Abbey in his *Present State*.[4]

Instead Edward Pugin was called on in 1864 to adapt the eighteenth-century house by adding a steep mansard roof and creating a large internal, two-storey hall and a chapel in the roof, and 'a spacious church ... Early English [was] also intended'.[5] Requisitioned in 1942, when the contents were sold and the archive destroyed, the house was demolished in 1964 and the rubble used as hard core for the M1 motorway.[6] The garden buildings by Phillipps's ancestor, also Ambrose Phillipps (1710–1737), an amateur architect, survive, including the Triumphal Arch, the Obelisk and the Temple of Vesta, which was converted into yet another chapel by E. W. Pugin in 1873.[7] Rather than the church projects, it was the scale and expense of rebuilding of Garendon, on which he managed to spend 'the income of three generations instead of that of life tenant', that overwhelmed Phillipps.[8]

1. E. S. Purcell, *The Life and Letters of Ambrose Phillipps de Lisle* (1900), II, pp. 286–7.
2. A. Wedgwood, *Catalogue of the Drawings collection of the RIBA, the Pugin family* (1977), pp. 58–9.
3. Pugin, *True Principles*, pp. 50–1, plate K, fig. III; R. O'Donnell, 'From "Old English Catholic Mansions" to "Castles in Connecticut": the country house practice of A. W. and E. W. Pugin', in M. Airs (ed.), *The Victorian Country House* (Oxford, 2000).
4. R. O'Donnell, 'Pugin designs for Downside', *Burlington Magazine*, 223 (1981), pp. 230–3.
5. *Tablet* (1864), p. 333; *Building News* (1864) p. 362; the E. W. Pugin-de Lisle correspondence, private collection, Leicestershire.
6. M. Airs (ed.), *The Victorian Country House*, pp. 88–9.
7. Magdalen College, Oxford, Archives, Bloxam MS no. 335, f. 70.
8. Purcell, *Phillipps*, II, p. 230.

GRACE DIEU MANOR

Ambrose Phillipps, like the 16th Earl of Shrewsbury, suffered from a mania for building. On his marriage to the Hon. Laura Clifford in 1833, Phillipps was given the Leicestershire estate of Grace Dieu, where the architect William Railton built a Tudor Gothic house and private chapel in 1833–4.[1] Railton's stucco faced rectangular-plan house faces the park. To the left, the porch tower was elaborated in its upper levels by Pugin with a clock face, battlements and spirelet and beyond it is the nave of the chapel extended to accommodate the public in 1837. To the right Pugin added the extensive two-storey service range with attics in 1847 (paid for by Phillipps's father) for the expanding family, and rearranged the service side of the house with a kitchen with a steep pitched roof, now internally subdivided and its lantern removed.[2] His additions make a text book contrast to what Pugin would have called Railton's 'all front' architecture. Further additions included a separate wing for the chaplain by 1848, and a services and stable court to the north, lower than the main house and with separate access, through a pair of gates under a pent roof with date – 1848 – and monogrammed 'AP' and 'LP'. Here Laura Phillipps distributed soup and clothes to the poor, and ran a small school.[3] Such was the house that housed the Phillipps and their sixteen children, one born each year between *c.*1834 and *c.*1850, until Ambrose inherited Garendon in 1862.[4] E. W. Pugin continued the relationship with work on the garden and other buildings.[5]

1. M. Pawley, *Faith and Family: The Life and Circle of Ambrose Phillipps de Lisle* (Norwich, 1993), p. 78; W. White, *Leicestershire* (1846), pp. 342–3.
2. Pawley, *Faith and Family*, p. 227.
3. M. Airs (ed.), *The Victorian Country House*, pp. 85–7.
4. Pawley, *Faith and Family*.
5. Purcell, *Phillipps*, II, p. 314.

THE CHAPEL AT GRACE DIEU

The chapel at Grace Dieu was built in three phases; the first part in 1834 (which became the chancel), the second, the current nave, in 1837,[1] and the third, the north aisle, in 1848–9. The chapel is faced in stucco with stone dressings, and surprisingly these finishes were continued by Pugin in 1848–9. Railton was architect of the first phase, and perhaps of the second, the four-bay nave with its massive Queen-post trussed roof.[2] The Jesuit Fr Randall Lythgoe was also consulted and there are similarities between the high altar here and a documented example at Princethorpe, by J. J. Scoles, his favourite architect, although both are now destroyed. It was Lythgoe who advised Phillipps to extend the chapel and use it as the basis for his proselytizing mission.[3] Phillipps installed what was reputed to be the first Catholic rood screen erected since the Reformation.[4] Pugin, who just missed the opening, arrived in November 1837,[5] and was from then on constantly altering and re-furnishing the interior, remaking the rood screen and chancel arch *c.* 1840, and adding flanking side altars and a pulpit.[6] In 1848–9 he opened a three-bay arcade to a north aisle, with generous three-light Decorated windows.[7] His beautiful stone baldachin survives here, with the crucifixus figure and cross from the former rood screen.[8]

Phillipps's piety and his alliances with the Catholic aristocracy are reflected in the installation of much decoration in the chapel in the 1840s and 1850s, such as stained glass and memorial brasses, all self-consciously dynastic. The glass on the south side of the nave (1853) is in memory of the 16th Earl of Shrewsbury who made Phillipps his executor and residuary legatee (although he ultimately did not receive the inheritance).[9] Supplied through E. W. Pugin to J. H. Powell's design, and incongruously labelled as to the 'XVII Earl', its drawing and rich colouring survive well.[10] Phillipps had to give up Grace Dieu before his death,[11] but the church and its furnishings survived, although the chancel was truncated *c.* 1900.[12]

In 1933 Grace Dieu passed to the Rosminian Order, who ran it as a preparatory school. A 1965 re-ordering of the chapel proved to be a piece of wilful and wanton iconoclasm paralleled by the contemporary stripping out of St Chad's Cathedral, Birmingham.[13] The pulpit, both side altars and their paintings, the rood screen, the painted, gilt-wood high altar and reredos, and the architectural frame of the altarpiece were all destroyed or disposed of. The side altar paintings ended up with the local car dealer: one has since been returned; the other now belongs to the Californian singer, Cher. They were said to be by the German Nazarene painter, Franz Ittenbach; an example of his work survives in the house, of St Thomas Becket and St Edward the Confessor. Larger canvasses formerly in the hall, by Kenelm Digby, can no longer be traced. In the denuded sanctuary, the new, deliberately primitive altar table was made up by using the consecrated altar stones of the side altars as uprights and the mensa of the former high altar as the new holy table. The icon of the Virgin, formerly behind the high altar, lost its architectural framing and was relegated to a secondary position. The Pugin sedilia (1848?) were removed, although an Easter sepulchre survives, probably because 1960s liturgical reformers did not know what it was for.

1. W. White, *Leicestershire* (1846), pp. 342–3.
2. Pawley, *Faith and Family*, pp. 91–2.
3. Jesuit Archives, Farm St, London, 'College of St Ignatius 1750–1874', f. 213: Fr Lythgoe to the Jesuit Provincial 23 May 1835, referring to an invitation to Grace Dieu.
4. Purcell, *Phillipps*, I, pp. 107–8.
5. Ibid., II, pp. 213, 288–93. Pugin twice referred to this rood screen as the first erected in England since the Reformation: *Present State* (1843) pp. 25, 142. Pugin's Diary, 24–7 November 1837, in Wedgwood, *Pugin Family*, pp. 38, 79.
6. Drawings by Pugin for the refitting of the chancel dated to 1841 (Purcell, *Phillipps*, II, pp. 288–9; Stanton, *Pugin*, p. 200) are in a private collection. Of the seventeen chapel drawings in the Myers Family Album, only one is dated 1848.

7. Pugin's Diary, 1–2 May 1848, in Wedgwood, *Pugin Family*, pp. 64, 96; *Weekly & Monthly OJ* (1849), 441.
8. The screen was removed in 1962: R. O'Donnell, Tour notes for the Pugin Society (July 1997).
9. Pawley, *Faith and Family* (1993), pp. 262–76.
10. Birmingham City Archives, Hardman Collection, Glass Day Book (1845–53), 4 October 1853, £145.; Metalwork Day Book (1849–53), f.546, altar furniture orders via E. W. Pugin, 8 June 1853.
11. *Oscotian* (1888), p. 112; Purcell, *Phillips*, II, pp. 368–9.
12. M. Airs (ed.), *The Victorian Country House*, pp. 86–7.
13. Ibid., p. 87, note 88.

THE GRACE DIEU ESTATE

Phillipps's passionate proselytism was not confined to the chapel at Grace Dieu but extended to local villages and into the grounds, where he held one of the first public Corpus Christi processions in England since the Reformation.[1] By 1842 there was a chapel in the woods,[2] fourteen Stations of the Cross[3] and a massive 17ft high public Calvary at Turrylog, all by Pugin[4] and consecrated in 1843.[5] At the foot of the Calvary was a school for 200 children.[6] None of these survives in its original site. Such buildings were in direct descent from the picturesque gardening of the eighteenth century, which attempted to recreate the scene and mood of antique sites seen during the Grand Tour (and of which Garendon Park was an example). Phillipps instead evoked the Catholic Tyrol and Bavaria, where on a tour in 1844 he ordered the carved Pieta figures for the chapel in the woods.[7] Two other missions had chapels opened in 1837, at Whitwick[8] and Mount St Bernard's,[9] and a church and school at Shepshed in 1842, all supported by Phillipps.[10]

1. *OJ*, IV (1837), 381–2; Purcell, *Phillipps*, II, pp. 289, 312–13. Further processions took place in October 1837: *OJ*, V (1837), pp. 282–5.
2. *Catholic Magazine*, NS, I, (1843), pp. 122, 355–60.

3. White, *Leicestershire* (1846), pp. 342-3.
4. *Catholic Magazine*, NS, I, (1843); White, *Leicestershire*, pp. 342-3.
5. *Tablet* (1843); p. 117; Pawley, *Faith and Family*, pp. 150-1.
6. White, *Leicestershire*, p. 343.
7. Pawley, *Faith and Family*, p. 222.
8. *OJ*, V (1837), 282-5; *Catholic Directory* (1838), pp. 37-9; Purcell, *Phillipps* I, p. 103.
9. See below; *Catholic Directory* (1838), p. 35.
10. See below; M. Airs (ed.), *The Victorian Country House*, pp. 87-8.

GREAT MALVERN, OUR LADY AND ST EDMUND

The Douai Benedictines, threatened with exile from France (which did not take place until 1902) came here in 1891. They commissioned Peter Paul Pugin to build a double nave church (1904-5) in his characteristic hammer-dressed stone with large, flush tracery windows.[1] Closed by the Benedictines in 1996, it was sold to Malvern College, the very elaborate furnishings having been disposed of beforehand, although the altar tomb of Archbishop Scarisbrick, OSB,[2] and the Stations of the Cross, in P. P. Pugin's style, survive.

1. N. Pevsner, *Worcestershire* (Hardmondsworth, 1977), p. 167.
2. William Scarisbrick, OSB (1828-1908), Bishop of Port Louis, Mauritius, was made Archbishop on his retirement in 1888.

HENLEY-ON-THAMES, SACRED HEART

The private chapel (1850-1) of Danesfield House in Buckinghamshire[1] was a late but important commission for A. W. Pugin from Charles Robert Scott-Murray MP (1818-1882), a personal friend.[2] He became a Catholic in 1844 and paid for the Pugin church at Great Marlow (1845-8).[3] The chapel continued to be embellished throughout the 1850s and 1860s and when Danesfield was demolished many fittings were saved, notably the high altar, the east window and the font, to be incorporated in the new church at Henley by A. S. G. Butler (1936).[4] By July 1852 E. W. Pugin was responsible for the orders both for metalwork and stained glass, and his name appears as 'architect, Birmingham, for Danesfield church', in the Hardman archive;[5] he claimed the whole commission as his in the *Catholic Directory* (1856).[6] The high altar has tall outer niches and figures of St Charles Borromeo and St Elizabeth based on A. W. Pugin's drawings,[7] and while the altar itself is closely based on the 'open altar' in Pugin and Smith's *Glossary of Ecclesiastical Ornament*,[8] it is largely the work of E. W. Pugin. It has marble columns supporting the mensa, closed at the back by a solid plinth supporting two sets of gradines or shelves for candles either side of the rectangular marble tabernacle decorated with coloured gem-like roundels. Beneath the mensa is a gilt wood and brass reliquary chest containing relics of St Calixtus brought back from Rome, attributable like the tabernacle doors to Hardman & Co. This 'open' ensemble, very similar to E. W. Pugin's now destroyed altar composition at Belmont,[9] was probably originally detached from the rich 'super altar' above it. The lower part has rectangular diapered tiles supporting a richly carved architectural and figured range, with a central figure of the Virgin and Child under a spire, with four nodding arches housing scenes of the life of St Charles Borromeo. This composition, the most important altar ensemble by E. W. Pugin to survive, is very similar to his contemporary high altar at Derby, and may be by the Birmingham sculptors Lane & Lewis;[10] certain of the bas-relief scenes are common to E. W. Pugin's designs at Ushaw College.[11] The magnificent east window to J. H. Powell's design with scenes from the life of the Blessed Virgin was shown at the London International Exhibition of 1862, when Hardman & Co. was awarded a bronze medal.[12] Panelling, moveable fittings and altar stuff from Danesfield were also incorporated here.

1. The house, demolished in 1908, is described in J. J. Sheahan, *History and Topography of Buckinghamshire* (1862), pp.

A. W. N. Pugin (1812–1852).
Portrait by J. R. Herbert, 1845.

John Talbot, 16th Earl of Shrewsbury and Waterford (1791–1852).
Portrait by Carl Blass, *c.* 1851.

The Alton Towers high altar *c.* 1840 (now at St Peter's Church, Bromsgrove).

Detail showing the 16th Earl of Shrewsbury with his patron, St John the Baptist, and the chapel at Alton Towers to the right.

St Mary's College, Oscott: the terrace front.

The chapel as furnished by Pugin 1837–8.

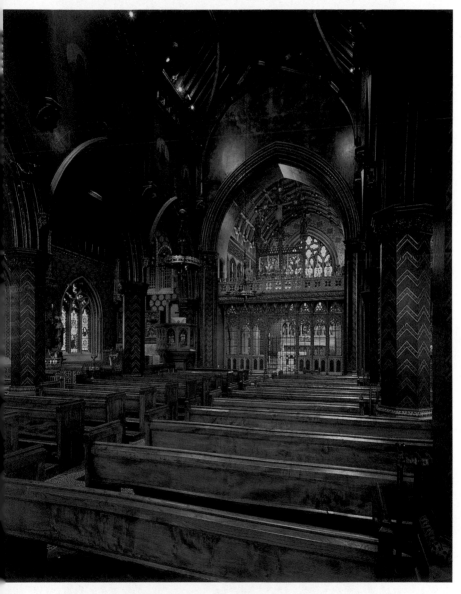

The Church of St Giles, Cheadle: the nave.

St Giles, Cheadle: the north or Lady aisle: wall painting and window – the Seven Corporal Works of Mercy – by William Wailes.

'Burying the Dead' from the Seven Corporal Works of Mercy.

The Rood.

Reredos detail.

St Giles, Cheadle: the pulpit and Lady altar.

The Blessed Sacrament chapel screen by Hardman & Co. to Pugin's design (1846), seen
from the baptistery aisle.

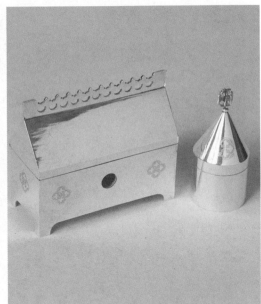

Above left:	Chalice, parcel gilt metal, enamels and jewellery, by Hardman & Co. to a Pugin design *c*. 1850 (Church of Our Lady, Blackmore Park, Worcestershire).
Above right:	St Giles, Cheadle: 'G[erman] S[ilver] plated Chrismatory, with two silver Bottles engraved £5 12s [and, right] a simple d[itt]o with silver £2.0.0.' 1846, by Hardman & Co. to Pugin's design. The first chrismatory is shown closed.

The first chrismatory with the lid open.

The staircase (*c.* 1848–50), Bilton Grange, Warwickshire. Probably by Myers'
workshop to Pugin's design.

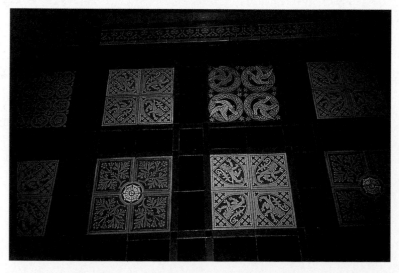

Encaustic floor tiles (1868), by Minton & Co., to J. H. Powell and E. W. Pugin's
design: Stanbrook Abbey.

Church of the Sacred Heart, Henley: high altar formerly at Danesfield. Tabernacle, mensa and reliquary. E. W. Pugin c. 1856.

Grace Dieu Manor: the north or Blessed Sacrament aisle (1848).

Church of St Mary, Wymeswold (Anglican): the nave seen through the chancel screen, as restored and furnished by Pugin (1845–50).

Church of St Mary, Warwick: the apse.

St Marie, Rugby: the interior of the E. W. Pugin church *c.* 1980.

Belmont, The Abbey Church of St Michael and All Angels.

Mount Saint Bernard Abbey: south front.

Belmont, school chapel.

Alton Castle (1843–56) from the Churnet Gorge.

All Saints, Barton-upon-Irwell, Manchester: detail of a wall painting by J. Alphege
Pippet of Hardman & Co., *c*. 1868, showing E. W. Pugin in medieval dress holding a
plan of the church.

906–7. Pugin's visits are noted in Wedgwood, *Pugin Family*, pp. 69, 90, and decorative arts designs listed pp. 190–1.

2. Scott-Murray was a prominent mourner at Pugin's funeral, and an executor of Shrewsbury's will.
3. *Tablet* (1845), p. 438; *OJ*, XXI (1845), 57–8. E. W. Pugin built the convent and schools (1854).
4. [Anon.] *The Catholic Church in Henley-on-Thames, 1275–1949, souvenir of the consecration ... 1949*; [*c*.1949]; O'Donnell, 'The Later Pugins', in Atterbury and Wainwright (eds), *Pugin*, p. 262.
5. Birmingham City Archives, Hardman Collection, Hardman Glass Order Book 1849–September 1852, under 31 July and 28 September 1852.
6. p. 232.
7. Pugin sketches are in the Myers Family Album.
8. 1844 edn, pp. 8–9, plate 71.
9. For Belmont see above.
10. For Derby see above.
11. O'Donnell, 'The Later Pugins', in Atterbury and Wainwright (eds), *Pugin*, p. 262.
12. G. Wallis, *The Art Manufactures of Birmingham and the Midland Counties in the International Exhibition of 1862* (1862), pp. 44–5.

HETHE, HOLY TRINITY

A charming 'Gothick' village church of 1832, with a house and school behind, it is typical in style and aspiration of the pre-Pugin Catholic 'chapel'. There is a stone altar and reredos and a font, all obviously to Pugin's design, but with no documentary evidence.[1]

1. J. Grant, *Hethe-with Adderbury, the story of a Catholic parish in Oxford* (Archdiocese of Birmingham Historical Commission, 2000).

KENILWORTH, ST AUGUSTINE OF ENGLAND

Pugin's small brick church was in the grounds of Fieldhouse, the home of the widowed Mary Louisa Amherst and her pious family.[1] It was begun in 1841 as a nave and chancel with a presbytery, all built by George Myers.[2] The belfry was added in 1849, the nave lengthened and the north aisle added between October 1851 and January 1852, by the architect Gilbert Blount, who also added a presbytery,[3] an example of Pugin's being passed over in favour of an another Catholic architect working in his style.[4] The reason for the change of architect may have been the scandal caused when Pugin, then a widower, courted Miss Amherst, who in 1850 became a nun.[5] The charmingly diminutive church is in the Decorated style.[6] Pugin wrote that it 'looks very old. It did not cost more than [£] 470 & has screen and font and altar all compleat.'[7] Although the rood screen was taken down in the 1970s, the statues of the Blessed Virgin and St John are now against the nave north wall; the crucifix in the chancel arch is probably that which Pugin described as 'a very nice crucifix of the early part of the 15th century.'[8] His altar was re-used, and recent stencilled decoration of the chancel walls and roof are a successful evocation of Puginesque design.[9] The east window to St Augustine of 1841 is by Wailes.[10] The Amherst family is commemorated in a brass on a black marble slab now fixed against the north aisle wall,[11] and in a window of 1869 by Hardman & Co. with the inscription to 'William Kerrill Amherst (died 1835); his widow, the builder of the church, Mary Louisa Amherst (died 1871); their son, Bishop Francis Kerrill Amherst of Northampton, and their daughter Mother Mary Barbara Amherst' and other family members, all with their patron saints.[12]

Pugin wrote very tartly to Mrs Amherst about the fixing of the wayside crucifix in 1842: 'My Dear Madam, To my great mortification I have just learnt that the cross in your cemetery has been set up contrary to my directions . . . the ends of the cross instead of standing N & S are [placed?] east and west contrary to the practice of all Christendom.'[13]

1. *Tablet* (1904), p. 473.
2. Belcher (ed.), *Letters of Pugin*, I, pp. 248-9, Pugin to F. K. Amherst, 29 June 1841.
3. A view signed 'G. R. B. 1849' in BAA, P182/T4, shows his project; his presbytery plan is P182/T7.
4. [By a member of the community], *Life of Mother Mary Agnes Amherst* (Exeter, 1927).
5. Belcher (ed.), *Letters of Pugin*, I, p. 279; BAA, P182/5/3, Mary Louisa Amherst's diary, f. 6. But Pugin had undercharged, and later sent in for extras.
6. A bird's-eye sketch, not by Pugin, shows its original scale: BAA, P182/T5.
7. Belcher (ed.), *Letters of Pugin*, I, p. 293. See ibid., pp. 358 (note 3), 400 (note 8), for other furnishings such as the screen (in the priest's garage in 1976) and cruets, candlesticks, crucifix and tabernacle by Pugin, noted by this writer in 1976, but not identifiable by Brian Andrews in 2000.
8. Belcher (ed.), *Letters of Pugin*, I, p. 279.
9. E. Meaton, *The Church of St Augustine of England* (Kenilworth, 1998).
10. Belcher (ed.), *Letters of Pugin*, I, p. 279 (note 2).
11. D. Meara, *A. W. N. Pugin and the Revival of Memorial Brasses* (1983), pp. 112-13.
12. Dame Mary Francis Roskell, OSB, *Memoirs of Francis Kerrill Amherst, D. D.*, ed. H. Vaughan (1903), pp. 272-3.
13. BAA, R872, Pugin to Mrs Amherst, 2 May 1842; in Belcher (ed.), *Letters of Pugin*, I, pp. 344-5.

LEADENHAM, ST SWITHIN

In 1841 Pugin painted the roof of the Anglican church of St Swithin in Lincolnshire in rich polychromy of blues and reds with texts in Latin taken from the Litany and the Holy Communion service[1] for Bernard Smith (1815-1903), who was vicar from 1839 to 1842 when he resigned to become a Catholic. He finally served as priest at the Pugin church at Great Marlow for almost fifty years.[2] He co-operated with Pugin in the production of the *Glossary of Ecclesiastical Ornament* (1844).

1. Pugin's Diary, 31 August 1841, in Wedgwood, *Pugin Family*, pp. 49 (note 19), 86.
2. W. H. Gordon Gorman, *Converts to Rome* (1910), p. 253.

LINCOLN, BEDE HOUSES

The St Anne's Bede Houses (1847–50) were an Anglican foundation by the colourful figure the Revd Waldo Sibthorpe, who converted to Catholicism in 1841 and was ordained priest in 1841 but returned to the Anglican Communion in 1843.[1] The building is related to Pugin's designs, but as he explained: 'I never acted as architect ... but only supplied drawings from directions conveyed through Mr Myers'; it was executed without his supervision by Myers.[2] The chapel is by Butterfield.[3]

1. Richard Waldo Sibthorpe (1792–1879); he briefly became a Catholic again in 1865.
2. Pugin to J. R. Bloxam 2 January 1850: quoted in R. D. Middleton, *Magdalen Studies*, (London, 1936), p. 213.
3. N. Pevsner, J. Harris and N. Antram, *Lincolnshire* (Harmondsworth, 1989), p. 511.

LONGTON, STOKE-ON-TRENT, ST GREGORY

E. W. Pugin's church and presbytery of St Gregory, built under the supervision of the future Bishop Isley in 1868–9, one of most important churches in the diocese, was demolished and replaced by the present church in 1970. Bishop Isley's church was estimated for £5,000, but cost £7,000; it was consecrated in 1887. E. W. Pugin's church itself replaced the previous existing Lane End chapel.[1]

1. M. F. Newbon, *This Potter's Clay, A History of St Gregory's Parish Longton* (Stoke-on-Trent, 2000); *Irish Builder* (1867), p. 237; *Builder* (1868), pp. 200, 498; (1869), pp. 468, 632–3; *Building News* (1868), pp. 152 (1869), p. 77; *Victoria County History of Staffs.* VIII, p. 273.

MOUNT ST BERNARD ABBEY

The building of Mount St Bernard Abbey by Ambrose Phillipps was conceived as a reparation for the destruction of the monasteries at the Reformation in general, and of the Cistercian Garendon Abbey by his own ancestors in particular, and was to be the culmination of his *manie-de-batir*. He built two monasteries, the first by William Railton 1835–7,[1] and the second by Pugin (1840–4) on a different site. An Irish Cistercian monk visited Grace Dieu in 1833,[2] and in 1835 Phillipps asked the Irish Cistercians to make a foundation, on land given by him and with some financial help from Bishop Walsh.[3] The first monks arrived 29 September 1835 and the first church and house was opened on 11 October 1837 to the design of William Railton. Although a complete monastery 'in the Elizabeth style'[4] was built, it was soon too small. Typically there was a misunderstanding by Phillipps as to what the monks were actually for. Shrewsbury wanted a foundation of Christian Brothers, that is a teaching order, while Phillipps thought that the monks could serve his missions, which they initially agreed to do.[5] Phillipps's first chaplain was a somewhat peripatetic Cistercian monk, Dom Woolfrey. The still sceptical Shrewsbury however agreed to visit and suggested a more picturesque site (which Phillipps had earlier considered). He made an offer of £2,000 on the condition that the work should begin on the new site, and that Pugin should be the architect.[6] It was in the incomplete church that Phillipps was buried in 1878.[7]

Pugin made fresh designs, dated 1839, and work began on the new site in 1840. A monastic quadrangle, a house for the relief of the poor, a kitchen, a calefactory (the roof of which was later raised), an infirmary 'in a style somewhat more ornamental than the earlier part' with a separate forward range forming lodges for strangers, effectively forming two cloisters, was begun. Pugin claimed to the Earl of Shrewsbury: 'It is one of the cheapest buildings ever built ... Mr Phillips['s'] ... little work on the Monastery will appear as soon as my woodcuts are ready', referring to *An Appeal to the Catholics of England on behalf of the Abbey Church of St Bernard,*

Charnwood Forest, Leicestershire.[8] Pugin was more practical
than Phillipps, who, trying to persuade Shrewsbury to adopt
the scheme, spoke of £400 in hand and only £2,000 needed:
'To complete their monastery would not take anything like
what Pugin says ... [and] Pugin gives all his time, drawings
etc. gratis and charges no percentages of the outlay ... with
materials so close at hand we shall be able to astonish every-
one with what he will build for.'[9] Even with Shrewsbury's
financial help Phillipps had to borrow £4,000 from Bishop
Walsh. To the north Pugin designed a church, the nave and
aisles of which were begun on 26 June 1843, but not the crossing tower and spire, transepts and Lady Chapel for which
Pugin's bird's-eye view, interior drawing and description
published firstly in the *Appeal* and then in *Present State*.[10] The
nave and house were blessed on 20 September 1844.[11]

Once the church was built, Phillipps found himself in
disagreement with the monks, who wished to close it to external worshippers, and in 1849 they gave up work on the
mission and affiliated to the French Cistercian Order. On 17
February 1849 Dom Palmer was consecrated as the first full
abbot in England since the Reformation, and Pugin designed
a mitre for him, the gift of Phillipps.[12] E. W. Pugin built the
chapter house *c*.1860.[13] The church was re-orientated in
1935–9 by F. J. Bradford, architect, and the crossing tower
added in a post-Second World War rebuilding by the Leicester architect Albert Herbert, so that Pugin's nave now forms
the monastic choir, which is not accessible to the public.[14]
None of the current fittings is associated with him.

The site of Mount St Bernard's is highly picturesque, the
monastery lying below the rocks on which a Calvary was built
in 1847. It was recorded in a painting showing the buildings 'as
completed' by the Catholic convert painter and friend of Pugin,
J. R. Herbert, in 1862. It attracted many visitors, and queues of
carriages, as the only working example of a monastery in
England, since Downside and Ampleforth did not begin regular
monastic life in their buildings until the last decade of the nineteenth century. The original Railton buildings were converted
into a Catholic reformatory[15] (which did not prosper). In the

twentieth century, the Pieta chapel, formerly at Grace Dieu,[16] was re-erected here but with simplified details *c.*1950.

1. A. C. Lacey, *The Second Spring in Charnwood Forest* (Leicester, 1985), pp. 12–18.
2. The mainly English monks came from Melleray in France and Mount Melleray in Ireland: Revd Ailbe J. Lubby, *The Story of Mount Melleray* (Dublin, 1952 edn); Pawley, *Faith and Family*, pp. 85–8.
3. Purcell, *Phillipps*, I, pp. 66–76.
4. [Dom Bernard Palmer], *A Concise History of the Cistercian Order by a Member of that Order* (London, 1852), p. 278; Pawley, *Faith and Family*, pp. 88–9, 93–4.
5. Pawley, *Faith and Family*, pp. 69–70, 81–84.
6. [Palmer], *Cistercian Order*, pp. 280–2; Purcell, *Phillipps*, I, pp. 76–8; Pawley, *Faith and Family*, pp. 193–4.
7. Pawley, *Faith and Family*, pp. 390–1.
8. Belcher (ed.), *Letters of Pugin*, I, pp. 178–9; Ambrose Phillipps and John Talbot, *An Appeal to the Catholics of England on behalf of the Abbey Church of St Bernard, Charnwood Forest, Leicestershire* (1842).
9. Purcell, *Phillipps*, I, pp. 76–8. Pugin's drawings referred to in B. Little, *Catholic Churches since 1623* (1966), p. 237, then at the monastery, are now at Leicester Record Office. At Mount St Bernard's there is an 1869 plan (not by Pugin), a sketch by Phillipps of the 1837 monastery, and photographs and prints.
10. 'Present State', *Dublin Review*, 12 (1842), p. 121; 1843 edn, plate 7 following p. 96, plate 8 following p. 98, and pp. 96–101.
11. Purcell, *Phillipps*, II, pp. 367–8.
12. Palmer, *Cistercian Order*, p. 297; Lacey, *The Second Spring in Charnwood Forest*, pp. 19–29.
13. *Tablet* (1856), p. 503.
14. N. Pevsner and E. Williamson, *Leicestershire and Rutland* (Harmondsworth, 1984), pp. 323–6.
15. *Tablet* (1863), p. 23; Pawley, *Faith and Family*, pp. 303–4.
16. White, *Leicestershire* (1846), pp. 242–3 (under Grace Dieu); *Tablet* (1844), p. 532 referring to the Pieta chapel (first erected in 1837), but this structure and its Pieta group are of 1844. The Calvary figures are mid-twentieth century sub Eric Gill. Pugin's drawings for the 1843 Pieta Chapel at Grace Dieu are in the Myers family album.

NOTTINGHAM, ST BARNABAS' CATHEDRAL

Nottingham Cathedral (1842–4) was, after St Chad's Birmingham, Pugin's second great church commission in the Midlands, by then organized for Catholic purposes as the Central District. The congregation had provided itself with a new chapel in 1825–8, by the Lincoln Catholic architect E. J. Willson[1] for his brother, the priest Robert Willson.[2] Robert bought a large town centre site for a new church, and it was Pugin rather than his brother[3] who got the commission when Bishop Walsh decided to build a much larger church. The Bishop provided £3,500 and Lord Shrewsbury promised £7,000 for a brick church without a tower in the lancet style. Its nave and aisles were based, as a homage to Lord Shrewsbury, on the ruined Croxden Abbey in Staffordshire, a Cistercian house founded by a de Verdun ancestor.[4] Pugin attracted further funds to build in sandstone[5] and to add an elaborate east end with a crossing tower.[6] He had to defend both against a sceptical Shrewsbury, who complained to Bishop Walsh: 'The great central tower and five chapels are quite beyond our wants. He thinks all Oxford has already come over.'[7] There is evidence that Bishop Walsh intended to move his residence and headquarters here, so that a large brick presbytery was built with prominent 'TW' monograms.[8]

St Barnabas' is Pugin's most important surviving work in the Early English style. The plan has a long low nave and aisles, transepts and crossing, a chancel with an ambulatory round its three sides built over a crypt, and three projecting chapels; the crossing tower and spire presiding over the whole makes a highly effective east end massing. The materials are local sandstone and green Westmorland slate for the roofs. The building is squat in proportions, with a five-bay nave and four-bay chancel. As first completed with its Wailes stained glass windows and elaborately decorated east end it had, according to Pugin, '3 times the solemnity of St George's [Southwark]',[9] but he was later to find it too dark.[10] Pugin's letters to Lord Shrewsbury defending his concept of the church and its decoration are revealing, and he made minute estimates for all of the decoration and furnishing.[11] He wrote: 'How can your Lordship say that Nottingham will be bare . . . only think of the intricate perspective views pillar beyond pillar screen beyond Screen.'[12] He described it in *Present State* and made a detailed engraving of the chancel decoration.[13] The church was consecrated by Wiseman in 1844; Shrewsbury attended, but Pugin was absent because of his wife's death.[14] It became a cathedral in 1850 with the creation of Nottingham diocese.

Thereafter it was perhaps the least appreciated of his cathedrals, and little of its character has survived the many re-arrangements by bishops who played havoc with Pugin's arrangements, particularly the ex-Oratorian Bishop Brindle (1901–15) who demolished the rood screen and high altar. Much was restored by the architect F. A. Walters for Bishop Dunne in 1926–32,[15] only to be unpicked by Bishop Ellis with the architects Weightman & Bullen in 1961–2, who replaced the high altar with his own throne and placed a new altar in the crossing.[16] Further uninspired alterations for the liturgical reforms followed; the most recent re-ordering (1994) and furnishing is by Smith & Roper who have made an attempt at re-integrating the interior with appropriate colours, stencilling and encaustic tiled floors,[17] which goes some way towards reversing the 'bare barn' interior which Shrewsbury warned against.[18] Today only the Blessed Sacrament chapel as redecorated in 1933 by J. Alphege Pippet gives a hint at the intended character.[19] The three east end chapels retain their simple Pugin stone altars and wall arcades.

1. H. M. Colvin, *A Biographical Dictionary of British Architects 1600–1840* (1995 edn), pp. 1061–2.
2. Belcher (ed.), *Letters of Pugin*, I, pp. 377–8. He left in 1844 to be first Catholic Bishop of Hobart, Tasmania.
3. Pugin earlier had to apologize for taking the St Mary, Derby, commission from him: ibid., p. 80.
4. Ibid., pp. 289–93.
5. Ibid., pp. 303–4, 306.
6. Ibid., p. 290.
7. Ibid., pp. 294–5; 303–4, 306; BAA, B606, Shrewsbury to Walsh, 16 November 1841.
8. *Tablet* (1848), p. 691.

9. Belcher (ed.), *Letters of Pugin*, p. 321.
10. A. W. N. Pugin, *Some of the Articles which have recently appeared in the 'Rambler' relative to Ecclesiastical Architecture and Decoration* (1850), p. 12.
11. Belcher (ed.), *Letters of Pugin*, I, pp. 291–2.
12. Ibid., p. 308.
13. nos. 1–3, following p. 62.
14. *OJ*, XIX, (1844), 143–4; *Tablet* (1844), pp. 550, 564, 579–80.
15. *Tablet* (1926), pp. 304–5.
16. B. Little, *Catholic Churches since 1623* (1966), p. 203; M. Cummins, *St Barnabas, Nottingham*, pp. 41–51.
17. J. Smith, 'The re-ordering of the Cathedral church of St Barnabas, Nottingham, an architect's account', in *Church Building*, 25 (1994), pp. 36–41; R. O'Donnell, 'A Passion to Build Places of Worship: Pugin cathedrals at Nottingham and Newcastle', *The Universe*, 'Our Heritage' supplement, 21 August 1994.
18. Belcher (ed.), *Letters of Pugin*, I, p. 81.
19. *Catholic Herald*, 25 February 1933.

NOTTINGHAM, MERCY CONVENT

The third part of the large site bought for the Cathedral and presbytery at Nottingham[1] was occupied by the large quadrangular Mercy Convent by Pugin (1844–6). This was another foundation from Handsworth. Pugin's red-brick building with stone dressings and slate roof is a much more confident and mature statement than Handsworth, and is an example of the ease with which he planned and composed institutional buildings in his mid-career. The long, multi-storey elevation towards the cathedral, with the gable and large Decorated window of the chapel expressed high up on the façade, is masterly. Pugin built the two-storey entrance elevation to College Street, the return facing the cathedral consisting of parlours on the ground floor and nuns' cells above, and the chapel, the body of which is part of the Derby Road elevation. The cost of £4,000 came from John Exton of Eastwell, Nottinghamshire. This range was heightened in 1857, when the west side of the quadrangle was closed in, with the costs met by Miss C. Whitgreave.[2]

The chapel had a rood screen and stalls arranged choir-wise, by Myers (1848)[3] (foolishly removed by the nuns in favour of moveable prayer desks *c*.1980), and a fine Hardman east window of 1847.[4] These were paid for by Miss Vavasour, who became a nun.[5] The convent has now closed but proposals for further removals have been resisted; the Nottingham architects, Wilkinson, Hindle, Halsall Lloyd Partnership are adapting it for housing.

1. *Tablet* (1848), p. 691.
2. [by a member of the Order of Mercy] *Leaves from the Annals, II*, pp. 327–33.
3. Birmingham City Archives, Hardman Collection, Decoration Day Book 1845–50, 1 November 1848, Myers woodwork at £37; the total charge was £177.
4. Ibid., Glass Day Book 1845–53, 22 April 1847, at £170.
5. *Leaves from the Annals, II*, p. 328.

PRINCETHORPE COLLEGE, OUR LADY OF THE ANGELS

English Benedictine nuns, who had fled from Montargis in France in 1792, bought Princethorpe in 1832 and began extensive buildings, including a chapel. Pugin was dismissive, writing to J. R. Bloxam in 1841: 'I am sorry [that] you were going to visit Princethorpe. It is a miserable specimen of the tawdry trashy taste of Modern religious. It is not even a ghost of an ancient nunnery.'[1] A. W. Pugin was not given any architectural work at Princethorpe although he designed (*c*.1850) a fine mahogany reliquary cross with silver plates, now at the Victoria & Albert Museum.[2] His son Peter Paul built the red-brick and stone-dressed church (1898–1901) in his most elaborate Decorated style, with steep pitched green Westmorland slate roofs. It was the gift of Hilda de Trafford, daughter of Sir Humphrey and Lady Annette de Trafford, themselves the donors of a series of churches by E. W. Pugin in Manchester.[3] The church has a complex plan, allowing the three different groups of enclosed nuns, schoolgirls and an 'extern' congregation housed in a transept to use it. There is a generous circulation route through a narthex and porches, side aisles and transepts. Enclosed within this was a monastic choir of stalls and abbess's throne in the nave, and beyond the transepts an ambulatory enclosing the magnificent sanctuary and high altar. The main accent is the metal rood screen, supporting wooden figures with the crucifix suspended above it; a complete series of metal screens enclose the sanctuary. The high altar has a prominent tabernacle with a socle for the monstrance with adoring angels, all in marble, a development of the 'benediction-altar' type. It is placed under a timber and metal baldachin with carved painted and gilt figures. Woodwork was one of P. P. Pugin's strengths and his wooden altars should be noted: in the transept of the Sacred Heart (with J. Alphege Pippet paintings); in the ambulatory to Benedictine saints (with Pippet paintings) along with a Pieta; and to St Joseph. There is also a marble altar to the Holy Child. The nuns have moved, but Princethorpe College occupies their buildings, and the church remains open for the local parish. It is one of Peter Paul Pugin's richest buildings, with some of his best surviving metalwork and woodwork furnishings.

1. Belcher (ed.), *Letters of Pugin*, I, pp. 140–1.
2. Metalwork Department, no. m.107–1978.
3. *A Short History of the Benedictines of St Mary's Priory, Princethorpe* (Ditchling, 1945); Frideswide Stapelton, OSB, *History of the Benedictines of St Mary's Priory, Princethorpe* (Hinckley, 1930). For the de Traffords, see under Rugby, St Marie.

RADFORD

Pugin's chapel of the Holy Trinity (1841) at Radford in Oxfordshire and a later convent and school attached are now private houses. The chapel built of local stone cost a mere £600.[1] It replaced the mission at Kidlington and was given by the Mostyn-Browne family.[2] This may be the 'Oxford church' referred to in Pugin's Diary in 1840.[3] In a letter of 1841 he wrote of including it in *Present State*, but did not do so.[4]

1. *Tablet* (1841), pp. 55, 137–8.
2. Mrs Bryan Stapleton, *Post-Reformation Catholic Missions in Oxfordshire* (1906), pp. 132–41.
3. Pugin's Diary, 11 May 1840, in Wedgwood, *Pugin Family*, (1985), pp. 45, 47, 84–5.
4. Belcher (ed.), *Letters of Pugin*, I, pp. 182–3.

RATCLIFFE COLLEGE

Ratcliffe College, the Catholic public school in Leicestershire formerly run by the Rosminian Order[1] and since 1996 headed by a lay headmaster, stands on an elevated site just off the Fosse Way six miles north of Leicester. It was opened as the novitiate of the Order and shortly became a school. Pugin's east-facing ranges of red brick with stone dressings and window tracery, and with slate roofs, were begun at the south in 1843–4, including the fine entrance tower,[2] a centre range formerly a chapel, and an 1848–9 north-end range, which included another chapel.[3] This fine frontage, derived from Pugin's rejected scheme for Balliol College, Oxford, made Ratcliffe one of the most impressive Catholic school or college building projects of the period, although it was only a fragment of what he had intended, and was published as a fund raising exercise.[4] C. F. Hansom was at work here in 1849,[5] taking over from Pugin but continuing his scheme and style in a collegiate layout with south (1854) and north (1857–8) ranges.[6] E. W. Pugin began work in 1862 on the Study range,[7] and despite a scheme to use his father's church as an ante-chapel,[8] he completed the quadrangle to the west with ranges either side of a soaringly high chapel (1866–7) to a different design.[9] Its west front has his typical tripartite entrance door, gallery, and rose window above. Despite E. W. Pugin's view that the church would cost £4,550,[10] a tender estimate of £3,400 was accepted.[11] Structural problems resulted, and Pugin refused to attend the opening. The interior had a fine E. W. Pugin altar, sculpted by R. L. Boulton,[12] and J. H. Powell rood screen and glass including the west window (1891).[13] However the church fell victim to the widespread mid-twentieth century anti-Victorian prejudice and the ambitions of the leading Catholic headmaster of the day, Fr Claude Leetham, who replaced it with a new chapel (1962–5) by J. Bower Norris, with important works of art by Jonah Jones.

1. C. Leetham, *Ratcliffe College, 1847–1947* (Leicester, 1949).
2. White, *Leicestershire* (1846), p. 431. Pugin's drawings (1844) for an unexecuted phase of this scheme are in the Ratcliffe Archives.
3. *Tablet* (1847), p. 374; drawings in the Myers Family Album. It was later converted into a museum and library.
4. R. O'Donnell, 'Extra Illustrations of Pugin's Buildings in T. H. King's "Les Vrais Principes"', in *Architectural History*, 44 (2001), 57–63.
5. Ratcliffe College Archives, correspondence C. F. Hansom to Fr Pagani referring to work begun 15 August 1849; however, the first payment to Hansom was dated 30 January 1850.
6. Leetham, *Ratcliffe College*, pp. 36–45.
7. *Tablet* (1863), p. 475.
8. Ratcliffe Archives, E. W. Pugin letters beginning with his estimate 25 September 1865. Pugin's chapel became the museum.
9. Ibid., Specifications 'New Church' May 1862 has 'taken down the wall between present chapel and the new building', f. 2. There are estimates for a 'Lodge' (May 1862) and 'New Offices' (June 1862).
10. Ibid., E. W. Pugin letters, 25 September, 1 November 1865.
11. Ibid., by Denny of Rugby, 8 November 1865.
12. Ibid., E. W. Pugin letter, 28 November 1866.
13. Ibid., J. Hardman & Co. invoice, £270, February 1891, and an earlier album of stained glass drawings.

READING, ST JAMES

For this neo-Norman style church (1837–40) Pugin built in the local flint, with stone dressings, prompted by the romantic association with the adjacent ruins of Reading Abbey about which he was initially enthusiastic.[1] It was to be paid for equally by James Wheble of Whiteknights, Reading, and by Bishop Walsh. Pugin also designed a presbytery based on the twelfth-century (so-called) Jew's House in Lincoln. But Wheble's death meant that it was not built, and that the internal decoration and furnishing of the church were not proceeded with (as Pugin complained to the priest).[2] Pugin later reacted against the neo-Norman style, which he went on to use at the crypt at St Chad's, and he gradually excluded this church from the canon of his buildings so that it does not appear in *Present State* or the frontispiece of the *Apology*. The church is so much rebuilt that little of Pugin's hand survives, except in the west front.[3] The church was extended with aisles and apse in the same style by the architect W. C. Mangan in 1926.[4]

1. *OJ*, V (1837), 405–8; *Catholic Magazine*, II (1838), pp. 61–3; NS IV (1840), p. 567; *Tablet* (1840), pp. 116, 176.
2. Belcher (ed.), *Letters of Pugin*, I, pp. 138–9.
3. 'St James Roman Catholic Church, Reading' illustrated and described in *Stranger's Guide to Reading* (1862).
4. [Anon.], *Brief History of St James Catholic Church and School*, c.1970.

RUGBY, ST MARIE

The small stone and slate roofed church by Pugin (1846–7) and his builder George Myers was given to the Rosminian Order c.1850. Of the original church, the west tower with a saddle-back roof, a nave and a chancel all survive, but a north porch and sacristy and a north or Lady Chapel were replaced (1863–4) by E. W. Pugin. A. W. Pugin built far fewer chuches after 1846, so that the evidence of the few late commissions which he received is worth studying. Opened on 8 September 1847, St Marie's was the gift of Captain John Hubert Washington-Hibbert of Bilton Grange, Rugby. His wife worshipped there, and he himself was to become a

Catholic in 1849. At the opening 'many Protestants [were] present, among them several boys from Rugby School'.[1] Pugin's sanctuary, with a rood screen and stalls to seat twenty, is now the Hibbert Chantry (originally housed in the Lady Chapel). The fine memorial brass by Hardman & Co. was commissioned to record the death in 1856 of Bertram Talbot, Mrs Washington-Hibbert's son by her first marriage, who became the 17th Earl of Shrewsbury; the figures of Captain Washington-Hibbert (who died in 1870) and Mrs Washington-Hibbert (died 1892), and kneeling children of both her marriages, were included at this time.[2] The glass here is post-1947 (following a fire), strongly coloured and drawn, figurative and dynastic, with the Hibbert arms. The altar is probably Pugin's original high altar. There is another fine Hardman brass in the north aisle to a convert member of the Wilberforce family. In this church was celebrated the wedding of Captain Washington-Hibbert's stepdaughter Lady Annette Talbot to Sir Humphrey de Trafford,[3] who in 1865 went on to build E. W. Pugin's most important English church at Barton-upon-Irwell, Manchester.[4]

E. W. Pugin's church (1863–4), also of stone, but handled quite differently from his father's, was added in two phases,[5] with sculpture by his favoured sculptor, R. L. Boulton of Cheltenham.[6] The commanding tower and spire (1871–2) was by E. W. Pugin's pupil Bernard Whelan (later a Rosminian), with striking sculpture, particularly the angels, by Theodore Phyffers.[7] It is one of the most important High Victorian churches in the diocese, and the interior survives remarkably intact, although J. H. Powell's wrought-iron rood screen was demolished in 1962. The magnificent high altar is by Donnelly, a Coventry architect, also carved by R. L. Boulton. The apse wall paintings (1908) by Hardman & Co. (designed by J. Alphege Pippet) have recently been restored.[8]

In front of the church is the boys' school by C. F. Hansom, opened in 1851, with the convent and girls' school (1853–4) on the north side of the cemetery, both of stone with slate roofs.[9] Behind the church is the former Rosminian novitiate, now St Wulstan's College, built by George Myers (1850–1) following a dispute between Pugin and Fr Pagani, the Rosminian Provincial; from certain details, such as the dormers and other window tracery, the architect may well be once again C. F. Hansom, who was thus supplanting Pugin.[10] The church makes a fine sight from the grounds of Rugby School, where in the nineteenth century it was known as the Tolly Church, tolly being the word for candle in the school argot.[11] Perhaps Rugby schoolboys crept into its candle-lit interior.

1. *Tablet* (1847), pp. 596–7; *Builder* (1847), pp. 448–9.
2. Birmingham City Archives, Hardman Collection, Metalwork Day Book (Dec. 1854–Dec. 1857) f. 348, 5 December 1856, £100.
3. *Illustrated London News* (1855), pp. 92–3.
4. R. O'Donnell, 'The Later Pugins', in Atterbury and Wainwright (eds), *Pugin*, pp. 266–7.
5. *Builder* (1864), p. 502; he also designed the former presbytery.
6. Boulton was also employed at Stanbrook.
7. *Builder* (1871), p. 339.
8. D. and L. Thackray, *A Brief History of St Marie's Church, 1844 to 1986* (1987), drawing largely on Fr Stephen Eyre Jarvis's *Guide* (*c.*1914).
9. C. F. Hansom was writing to Hardman about fittings for the church and for Bilton Grange (see below) by November 1852: Birmingham City Archives, Hardman Collection, Letters box, 1852.
10. *Builder* (1850), pp. 199, 226; *Architect and Building Operative* (1850), pp. 203, 227; *Tablet* (1851), p. 499.
11. Information from Hywel Williams.

RUGBY, BILTON GRANGE

This house, now a private school,[1] was the seat of Captain J. H. Washington-Hibbert who paid for the Catholic church in Rugby. A minor late-Georgian building, from 1841 it was altered progressively by Pugin, who added a great stair tower, a hall and kitchen offices, and a set of state rooms, which, as recently restored, give a sense of what the interiors at Alton

Towers were like.[2] The Hibberts left in 1860, and the house is now a preparatory school.

1. W. S. Blackshaw, *More than just a School: A History of Bilton School* (1985).
2. R. O'Donnell, 'From "Old English Catholic Mansions" to "Castles in Connecticut": the country house practice of A. W. and E. W. Pugin', in M. Airs (ed.), *The Victorian Country House* (Oxford, 2000), pp. 79–80.

SHEPSHED, FORMER CHURCH OF ST WINEFRED

Ambrose Phillipps borrowed £500 from Bishop Walsh and paid another £200 from his own funds to build a church (1841–2) with a school in the basement[1] to house the mission of his chaplain, the Italian Rosminian priest Luigi Gentili.[2] His missionary efforts were so successful that at one stage he was receiving groups of as many as 67 into the Church,[3] and by the time that the church opened in 1842 Phillipps was boasting to Shrewsbury that 'we now have more than one thousand converts in our villages'.[4] Pugin's church of nave and aisles under one roof pitch was built to this very tight budget, in the simplest local building stone, a hard Charnwood fieldstone; Myers's bill recorded in Pugin's Diary adding up to a mere £1,035.[5] Pugin also made minute estimates of the cost of the altar and sacristy furniture which he and Phillipps deemed essential.[6] In the event, Gentili did not serve the church here and the Rosminians gave up the parish to the diocese in 1852.[7] Another church was built on a different site in 1928, and after years of dereliction, this is now a private house and workshop.

1. Purcell, *Phillipps*, I, pp. 107–9.
2. C. R. Leetham, *Luigi Gentili, A Sower for the Second Spring* (1965), pp. 121–62.
3. Purcell, *Phillipps*, I, p. 107.
4. Ibid., pp. 109–110; II, p. 321.

5. Pugin's Diary, 18 May 1842, in Wedgwood, *Pugin Family*, pp. 52, 54, 87, 89.

6. Ibid., pp. 54, 89.

7. A. C. Lacey, *The Second Spring in Charnwood Forest* (Leicester, 1985), pp. 43–9.

SOLIHULL, ST AUGUSTINE

This church (1838–9) is built of local red brick with stone dressings and slate roofs. It was the first Pugin church to be opened, on 11 February 1839, with a High Mass celebrated by Dr Weedall.[1] John Hardman junior sang plainchant, and Pugin, typically advertizing himself, appeared carrying the processional cross. He also gave his architectural services free, a fact which he ensured was recorded in press reports.[2] Although these explained that 'even the very door hinges [are] Catholic',[3] that is Gothic, it is unclear whether the style of Pugin's original building was Early English or Perpendicular. At this date he was still designing in both styles, at Dudley and at St Chad's respectively. The east window of 1866 is in a Perpendicular style and attributable to J. H. Powell, and the windows of the nave were progressively altered in the 1880s to house Perpendicular-style stained glass by Hardman & Co., designed by J. Alphege Pippet.[4] In 1977 the north wall of the nave was demolished, so that the Pugin church became a western annexe of a larger building, further confusing the evidence. Pugin probably designed an Early English nave, with lancet windows but a 'Late' or Perpendicular chancel. The use of different styles was intended to suggest historic development in the building of the church, while the use of a more elaborate style for the chancel underlined its more sacred purpose. The chancel housed a late-medieval Flemish triptych and Perpendicular-style furnishings, such as the surviving wooden high altar which may have been made by the antique dealer and furniture maker Edward Hull.[5] Later alterations followed Pugin's Perpendicular style, beginning with the east window of 1866.[6] There was a sympathetic restoration in the

1930s by Hardman, Powell & Pippet to celebrate the centenary, no doubt on account of the continued residence of the Pippet family, chief designers to Hardman & Co., and prominent members of the parish.[7] By contrast the marriage of the original church with the 1970s extension is clumsy. The font and triptych are housed there, with Pugin's chancel forming a Blessed Sacrament chapel. The presbytery (1879) by J. A. Hansom & Son was then demolished.[8]

1. F. C. Husenbeth, *Life of R. R. Henry Weedall* (1860), p. 197; Bernard B. Malley, *Solihull and the Catholic Faith* (Birmingham, 1939), pp. 65–9.
2. *OJ*, IX (1839), 105.
3. Ibid., p. 65.
4. Birmingham City Archives Hardman Collection, Glass Book, 1866; Malley, *Solihull*, pp. 70–4. J. Alphege Pippet (1841–1903) lived at Lode Lane, Solihull: *Catholic Who's Who 1930*, p. 417; see also W. Covington, 'J. A. Pippet and Hardman Powell and Company', in *True Principles: The Voice of the Pugin Society*, Winter 2001, pp. 11–14.
5. Birmingham City Archives, Hardman Collection, Precious Metal Book, 1839, 'altar for Solihull, £18'.
6. This interpretation, based on historic photographs, was suggested to me by Brian Andrews.
7. Malley, *Solihull*, pp. 78–80. There was an early set of Hardman metalwork: Birmingham City Archives, Hardman Collection, Precious Metal Book, 1839, 23 January 1839, at £97, not now traceable.
8. Stanton, *Pugin* (1972), p. 197, gives the porch and sanctuary, improbably, to 'C. Hansom'. BAA, P249/6/19–20, has survey and proposal drawings signed 'G. Heveningham, April 1876'.

SPETCHLEY

Pugin chose local red brick for this Worcestershire 'school-chapel' of 1841, with blue-brick dressings and plain tiles. The simple vernacular structure shows that it was designed to be used as a school during the week and a chapel on Sundays and holy-days. The 'H'-plan has two cross-wings housing the two-storey schoolmaster's house in one and a schoolroom in the other, and another schoolroom in the centre. Both rooms have generous fireplaces and externally expressed stacks. A larger, traceried 'church' window in the gable, and the statue of St Nicholas in a niche and a rear porch-cum-sacristy show the chapel function.[1] This public chapel therefore removed the nuisance of public access to Mass in the magnificent two-storey chapel within Spetchley Park, by John Tasker.[2]

1. Pugin's Diary 29 September 1842, in Wedgwood, *Pugin Family*, pp. 48, 86.
2. H. M. Colvin, *A Biographical Dictionary of British Architects, 1600–1840* (1995), pp. 954–5; N. Pevsner, *Worcestershire*, (Harmondsworth, 1968), pp. 262–3.

STAFFORD, ST AUSTIN

E. W. Pugin made drawings for a new church in 1859,[1] but it was built in red brick with blue-brick dressings and slate roofs to a lesser scheme in 1861–2.[2] Both schemes were at right angles to and partly on the site of the small but precociously 'correct' Perpendicular Gothic style chapel of 1817–19, by the amateur architect Edward Jerningham (a member of the Catholic aristocratic family which supported the Stafford mission).[3] Pugin's friend, Francis Amherst, had been the priest there from 1856 to 1858. He then became Bishop of Northampton, where he commissioned a cathedral from Edward in 1860, only partly realized.[4]

1. BAA, APD/P255/1–6, six drawings for John Wyse, priest at St Austin's 1858–9.
2. *Builder* (1861), pp. 274, 326; 1862, pp. 553–4; *Building News* (1862), p. 75.
3. M. W. Greenslade, *St Austin's, Stafford* (Archdiocese of Birmingham Historical Commission, 1998), pp. 11–12.
4. Ibid., p. 12; *Builder* (1860), pp. 252, 480.

STAFFORD, BURTON MANOR

This house (1855–6) for Francis Whitgreave, was E. W. Pugin's first major domestic commission.[1] Built of red brick with stone dressings it was based on recollections of his father's house, St Augustine's Grange, Ramsgate (1843–4) which the Pugin family leased out 1852–62.[2] The Whitgreaves sold it in 1923, and Burton Manor now houses Stafford Grammar School; it is no longer a Catholic site.[3]

1. Birmingham City Archives, Hardman Collection, Metalwork Day Book (Dec. 1854–Dec. 1857), ff. 52–3, 21 February 1855, for E. W. Pugin's order for metal roof ridge details.
2. R. O'Donnell, 'The Kentish Obituary of Edward Pugin', in *True Principles: The Voice of the Pugin Society*, Summer 2000.
3. Information from the Revd M. Fisher (letter, 7 December 2001).

STANBROOK ABBEY, OUR LADY OF CONSOLATION

The convent of the English Benedictine nuns founded at Cambrai in 1625 was established here in Worcestershire in 1838 in purpose-built quarters.[1] E. W. Pugin, who was frequently employed by the Benedictine Order, built their red brick church (1869–71) and then cloisters to connect with the earlier buildings. The L-plan convent ranges are by P. P. Pugin (1878). E. W. Pugin first designed a west-end pinnacled bell-cote (his usual form) but here, unusually, a tower and spirelet were added, in a striking, variegated red and white brick with white stone dressings, vigorously polychromatic and in his most nervous, attenuated style. The buildings were roofed with Seddon's Patent Roman tiles. The church consists of choir and sanctuary under one roof-pitch, and the roof structure of closely set rib-arches rising from wall piers represents the first use of this form later to be characteristic of the practice. Arched windows are recessed between each major pier, and the stalls set back into them. The interior structure is stone faced, with fine carving by R. L. Boulton: E. W. Pugin called his angels 'perfection',[2] now unfortunately all painted over. E. W. Pugin's altar and reredos were installed in 1878, once again carved by Boulton.[3] The wrought-iron screen was approved by E. W. Pugin in June 1870 and made by J. H. Powell at a cost of £320.[4] There was also a hanging wooden, painted rood, another characteristic of later E. W. and P. P. Pugin church interiors. The glass was by Hardman & Co. The tiled floors (which E. W. Pugin and J. H. Powell took two days to design), were by Minton & Co. with the masterly use of deep black borders to draw the eye through the design.[5] These arrangements, first unpicked in 1936-7, were demolished, and the sanctuary floor levels altered, in the re-ordering of 1971 by Peter Falconer & Partners.[6] In the nave, the choir stalls and floor survive, as does the stained glass. The chapel of the Holy Thorn, with its altar by P. P. Pugin, also survives; here the tombs of Dom Laurence Shepherd, OSB, the chaplain who was almost E. W. Pugin's clerk of works, and some abbesses, are intact. Only the external chapel off the sanctuary is open to the public. It has a pair of transverse vaults, and a statue of St Benedict. The highly original iconography of the Sacred Heart and the Seven Sacraments windows are by J. H. Powell.[7]

1. *Stanbrook Abbey, a Sketch of its History 1625-1925* (1925).
2. Stanbrook Abbey Archives, E. W. Pugin to Shepherd, 16 May 1870; *Building News*, X (1868), p. 674; *Builder* (1871), p. 733; (1878), pp. 350-2.
3. *Irish Builder*, 13 (1871), p. 243.
4. Drawings in Birmingham City Archives, Hardman Collection; parts of the screen are in the Birmingham City Museum and Art Gallery.
5. Stanbrook Abbey Archives, Pugin to Shepherd, 17 October 1870.
6. A. Thompson and Sister Joanna Jamieson, OSB, 'Re-ordering of Stanbrook Abbey' in the *Clergy Review* (NS, LVII, no. 3, March 1972), pp. 241-8.
7. R. O'Donnell, 'Notes for the Pugin Society tour 12-16 July 2000'.

STONE, THE CHAPEL OF ST ANNE

Pugin's small, brick-built school-chapel (1843–4) survives in the garden of the Dominican convent, for which the large church by C. F. Hansom and Gilbert Blount was built later. The chapel is therefore the earliest relic of the Stone Catholic mission started by Blessed Dominic Barberi.[1] The cost was £600, some of it subscribed by a local man, James Beech.[2] The style was early Decorated, the only elaboration being the east window by William Wailes, with the figure of St Anne holding the child Virgin Mary, as a type for Christian education. The chancel had doors which could be closed to make the nave into a school (the hinges survive on the inner face of the arch), and the pews were said to tip up to form benches (as at St John's, Alton). With such diminutive, serviceable, matter-of-fact Gothic buildings, Pugin illustrates his revolutionary architectural thinking, as demonstrated in *True Principles* (1841), perhaps more clearly than in his more elaborate architecture. A surprisingly unsympathetic entry by Pevsner in *Staffordshire* misses this point, as well as dating the building to ten years later.[3]

1. Urban Young, CP (ed.), *Dominic Barberi in England, a new series of letters* (1935), pp. 88–93, 131.
2. *Tablet* (1843), p. 565.
3. N. Pevsner, *Staffordshire* (Harmondsworth, 1974), p. 268.

STONE, OULTON ABBEY, OUR LADY OF THE IMMACULATE CONCEPTION

This house belongs to the historic, but now sadly depleted, community of English Benedictine nuns founded at Ghent in 1624.[1] E. W. Pugin inherited the commission from his father, and it was one of his first works (1853–4).[2] A complete quadrangular layout, including the abbey church, was under discussion. His beautifully detailed and executed buildings in rich red sandstone with slate roofs are still in his father's

English Decorated style. The church has a nave and chancel under two roofs, of tall proportions and lit well by generous windows, especially the fine east and west windows. Internally, the walls are ashlared and the nave roof trefoil-shaped and panelled between ribs. Above the chancel arch are later-nineteenth-century paintings with figures by J. A. Pippet, and flanking carved statues. The arch retains its metal screen by J. H. Powell[3] and the reredos and altar are also original. The stalls and floors are of wood. It was consecrated in 1856.[4] As one of the most important Pugin sites in the diocese, it deserves to be far better known. The extern chapel is the only building accessible because of the enclosure.

1. *Annals of the English Nuns of Ghent, now at Oulton* (Oulton, 1894).
2. Birmingham City Archives, Hardman Collection Metalwork Day Book (Dec. 1854–Dec. 1857) f. 125, 10 July 1855; f. 324, 19 November 1856, attest to the importance of this scheme.
3. R. O'Donnell, 'Benedictine Building in the Nineteenth Century', in Dom Geoffrey Scott, OSB (ed.), *English Benedictine Congregation History Symposium*, III (1983), pp. 38–48.
4. *Catholic Directory* (1856).

STOURBRIDGE, OUR LADY AND ALL SAINTS

E. W. Pugin's church (1863–4) replaced an earlier building on the site. It is built in brick with stone dressings and has a nave and aisles; the tower and spire are by G. H. Cox after Pugin's design (1889–90).[1] The interior has E. W. Pugin's characteristic stumpy columns of Scottish granite on high plinths, with abstract capitals; the clerestory has cinquefoil windows, and the sanctuary has a rose window above an 1875 reredos. The very wide nave has a roof carried on a variation of his favourite truss, like a sort of giant ratchet. The proportions are tall and thin. The east end windows only are 1860s; the others are more recent, by Hardman & Co. There is a three-storey former convent and two-storey presbytery.[2]

1. *Builder* (1863), pp. 358, 393, 537; (1864), p. 10; *Tablet* (1863), p. 316; *Building News* (1889), p. 671.
2. T. Hand, *The Second Spring of Catholicity in Stourbridge* (Stourbridge, 1912).

STRATFORD UPON AVON, ST GREGORY THE GREAT

This new stone and slate church (1866) of nave, aisles and chancel is a typical example of E. W. Pugin's Geometric Gothic style.[1] The commission for the Benedictine mission at Stafford came from Dom Dunstan Scott, OSB, procurator of the Benedictine South Province, who had made tart comments on the work.[2]

1. *Building News* (1866), pp. 554, 719–20; *Builder* (1866), p. 893.
2. R. O'Donnell, 'Benedictine Building in the Nineteenth Century', pp. 38–48.

TUBNEY, ST LAWRENCE

A. W. Pugin had a small but interesting set of Anglican church commissions, usually restorations, but nothing like the number which his obvious skills deserved; his outspoken Catholicism made him unacceptable to Anglican sensibilities, except those of a handful of mostly clergy patrons. Of these, his favourite was undoubtedly the Revd J. R. Bloxam of Magdalen College, Oxford,[1] the patron of this Oxfordshire living. St Lawrence was Pugin's one complete new Anglican church. He complained of having to follow the rules of the local Anglican church-building charity, the Berkshire Church-Building Society, which demanded sufficient drawings and specifications to go out to tender, all of which Pugin avoided in his collaboration with George Myers.[2] Two schemes were involved, neither to the Church-Building Society's standard.[3] St Lawrence was built to a lesser scheme (1845–7) in beautiful local stone with stone-slate roofs. The style was

Decorated, and the scale diminutive.[4] Pevsner was dismissive: 'It is in no way distinctive and might be by anybody.'[5]

1. Above, p. 26.
2. Magdalen College, Oxford, Archives: Bloxam MS no.32, Pugin to J. R. Bloxam, n.d. but *c*.1845.
3. K. Triplow in *True Principles* (Newsletter of the Pugin Society), vol. 1 no. 5 (Winter 1997–8).
4. *Victoria County History of Berkshire*, IV, p. 380.
5. N. Pevsner, *Berkshire* (Harmondsworth, 1966), pp. 242–3.

UTTOXETER, ST MARY

Pugin's church (1838–9) was first altered by P. P. Pugin in the later 1870s, and then rebuilt by the architect Henry Sandy in 1913.[1] The west front bell-cote, gable and rose window are still identifiable, with a narthex, aisles, Lady Chapel and sacristies added to the cell of Pugin's church.[2] This building was of great importance to Pugin as one of his first new churches; there is much published evidence for the work of Pugin who himself described and illustrated it in the Catholic press,[3] and with a slightly different interior in *Present State*.[4] Pugin's working drawings for the church (1838) and the priest's house (1839), formerly in possession of the descendants of the builder John Bunn Denny,[5] one of Shrewsbury's employees, are much more elaborate than those he produced later for George Myers. At this early stage Pugin did not prescribe a screen but an arched rood beam. His altar is still in place, but his cylindrical 'tower' tabernacle is in storage.[6] His fascination with church furnishings included, in this case, the arcane proposal for a hanging pyx in which to reserve the Blessed Sacrament. Although Shrewsbury was a patron, George Morgan (priest here 1838–42 and later President of Oscott) is said to have 'sold his paternal estate to build the chapel'.[7]

1. P. F. Wilson, *St Mary's Catholic Church 1839–1989*.

2. N. Pevsner, *Staffordshire* (Harmondsworth, 1974), p. 290.
3. *OJ*, IX (1839), 33–6. See also ibid., pp. 118–19, 336; *Catholic Magazine*, III (1839), p. 701.
4. p. 36, plate xvi, p. 43.
5. Sotheby's catalogue *Early English Watercolours and ... Architectural Drawings* (30 April 1987), p. 103. They are now at the Getty Centre for the History of Art, Santa Monica, California.
6. Pugin, *Present State*, pp. 41–2, and information from Brian Andrews; Pevsner, *Staffordshire*, refers to sedilia as Pugin's.
7. B. W. Kelly, *Historical Notes on English Catholic Missions* (1907), p. 406; F. C. Husenbeth, 'The Very Rev. George Morgan, D. D.', in *Staffordshire Catholic History*, 18 (1988), pp. 25–6.

WARWICK, ST MARY IMMACULATE

This small church by E. W. Pugin of 1859–60, was built in cheap red and yellow brick with slate roofs but carefully planned to achieve a wide nave and apse, with only narrow 'passage' aisles, so that the whole congregation could see the altar.[1] Here he solved the problem of the reconciling of the Gothic style with the Tridentine liturgy, where seeing the altar (rather than hiding it behind a screen) was paramount. This plan was the model for the larger church of Our Lady of Reconciliation, Everton, Liverpool (1859–60), which he was building at the same time and which became the standard for the rest of his career.[2]

1. *Builder* (1859), p. 445.
2. R. O'Donnell, 'Later Pugins', in Atterbury and Wainwright, (eds), *Pugin*, pp. 264–5.

WOLVERHAMPTON, SS PETER AND PAUL

In this neo-classical church by John Ireland (1827–9) where Milner officiated, the second of Pugin and Hardman & Co.'s monumental brasses commemorating Bishop Milner (an adaptation from that shown at the Great Exhibition, 1851) can be found mounted incongruously on the wall.[1]

1. D. Meara, 'Monuments and Brasses', in Atterbury and Wainwright (eds), *Pugin*, pp. 194–5.

WOLVERHAMPTON, FORMER MERCY CONVENT

E. W. Pugin's brick ranges for the large former Mercy Convent (1860)[1] at SS Mary and John, Snow Hill, survive. However his church of St Patrick (1866)[2] was demolished and replaced by a building on another site *c*.1970.

1. *Builder* (1860), p. 244; [by a member of the Order of Mercy] *Leaves from the Annals, II*, pp. 341–2.
2. *Building News* (1866), p. 420; (1867), p. 365; *Builder* (1866), p. 514; *Irish Builder* (1866), pp. 223–4.

WYMESWOLD, ST MARY

Pugin's few Anglican commissions came from very independent-minded clergy patrons, in this case the Revd Henry Alford, vicar here 1835–53.[1] His church was six miles up the Fosse Way from Ratcliffe, and Pugin probably took on the commission because of this proximity. The medieval church was conservatively restored by Pugin from 1844 to 1850,[2] and the work is carefully recorded in *A History and Description of the Restored Parish Church of St Mary, Wymeswold, Leicestershire* (n.d., *c*.1850) where Alford's opinion of Pugin as 'the most eminent Architect of the day' is given.[3] It is interestingly reviewed in the *Tablet*.[4] Pugin rebuilt the chancel and the east window, and replaced the chancel and nave roofs; an attractive two-storey north porch (with a strong sense of E. W. Pugin's hand about it) and a south porch were added. The north and south aisles were refitted and much quarry and stained glass installed, including some of the first glass that Hardman produced.[5] The ten-light east window, however, looks like Wailes. Much Pugin furniture survives, in stone, such as the font in the south aisle, and in wood, such as the chancel screen and stalls and the panelling in the sanctuary, all oak coloured. However, little of the metalwork and stencilled texts and mottoes as described and illustrated in the *History*, survive.

1. Later Dean of Canterbury.
2. G. K. Brandwood, *Bringing them to their knees: church-building and restoration in Leicestershire and Rutland 1800–1914* (Leicestershire Archaeological and Historical Society and G. K. Brandwood, 2002), pp. 18–20, 52, 132.
3. p. 10, undated but *c.*1850; M. Belcher, *A. W. N. Pugin, an annotated critical bibliography* (1987), pp. 156–7, dates it to *c.*1846, which is too soon in the campaign to describe so much as achieved.
4. *Tablet* (1850), pp. 165–72.
5. Birmingham City Archives, Hardman Collection, Glass Day Book (1845–53), orders of 15 December 1845.

THE ARCHDIOCESE OF BIRMINGHAM HISTORICAL COMMISSION was set up early in 1984. Its main purpose is to encourage interest in the Catholic history of the Midlands by publishing well researched and readable books on subjects of special interest to Catholics of the area now covered by the Archdiocese of Birmingham.

Publications:
No.1: **Maryvale** by Beth Penny
(1985 – ISBN 1 871269 0 08)
No.2: **John Milner** by M. N. L. Couve de Murville
(1986 – ISBN 1 871269 01 6)
No.3: **Oscott** by Judith F. Champ
(1987 – ISBN 1 871269 02 4)
No.4: **St Chad's Cathedral, Birmingham** by Michael Hodgetts
(1987 – ISBN 1 871269 03 2)
No.5: **Those who have gone before us** by Marie B. Rowlands
(1989 – ISBN 1 871269 05 9)
No.6: **Midlands Catholic Buildings** by Michael Hodgetts
(1990 – ISBN 1 871269 04 0)
No.7: **Harvington Hall** by Michael Hodgetts
(1991 – ISBN 1 871269 06 7; 1998 – ISBN 1 871269 12 1)
No.8: **Saint Austin's, Stafford 1791-1991** by M W. Greenslade
(1991 – ISBN 1 871269 07 5; 1998 – ISBN 1 871269 13 X)
No.9: **St Aloysius' Parish, Oxford** by Fr Jerome Bertram
(1993 – ISBN 1 871269 08 3)
No.10: **St Chad of Lichfield and Birmingham** by M. W. Greenslade
(1996 – ISBN 1 871269 11 3)
No.11: **Father Hudson and his Society** by Sylvia M. Pinches
(1998 – ISBN 1 871269 14 8)
No.12: **St George's, Worcester 1590-1999** by Fr Brian Doolan
(1999 – ISBN 1 871269 15 6)
No.13: **Life at Harvington 1250-2000** by Michael Hodgetts
(2001 – ISBN 1 871269 17 7)
No.14: **The Pugins and the Catholic Midlands** by R. O'Donnell
(2002 – ISBN 1 871269 17 8)
No.15: **William Bernard Ullathorne** by Dominic Aidan Bellenger
(2001 – ISBN 1 871269 17 9)
No.16: **Hethe-with-Adderbury** by Joy Grant
(2000 – ISBN 1 871269 18 0)

Copies are obtainable from Archdiocese of Birmingham Historical Commission, Maryvale House, Old Oscott Hill, Kingstanding, Birmingham, B44 9AG (0121 3608118).